JEAN K. DOUGLAS

WHY I LEFT THE CHURCH,
WHY I CAME BACK,
AND
WHY I JUST MIGHT
LEAVE AGAIN

♣ FORTUITY PRESS ♣

Fortuity Press
www.fortuitypress.com
Astor, Florida

Printed in the United States of America.

Cover design by Jean K. Douglas and Alexander H. Douglas
Cover illustration by Kathryn R. Flint

TO MY MOTHER,
WHO DID HER BEST TO SHOW US THE WAY

AND

TO ALL THOSE IN THE CHURCH
WHO HAVE RESISTED RACISM
AND OPPRESSION IN ALL ITS FORMS

Why I Left the Church, Why I Came Back,

and

Why I Just Might Leave Again

by

Jean K. Douglas

CONTENTS

Acknowledgements	9
Preface	11

PART ONE: THE FORMATIVE YEARS

The Wedding	16
Confirmation	21
Altar Server	27
Unlikely Miracles	33
Confession	38
Bannings	42
The Rosary	49
Sex	55
Images	62
Intellectual Freedom	65
St. Jude	70
The Sermon	75
Transubstantiation	86
White Flight	90

PART TWO: LEAVING
The Doors Close   99
Leaving?   105

PART THREE: THE PRODIGAL SOUL
Faith Without Works   113
Another Sermon   119
New Faculty   124
Ministry for Black Students   127
You Just Don't Fit   132

PART FOUR: GOODBYE AGAIN?
The Letter   138
Why?   143
Conclusion   152
Work Cited   157

ACKNOWLEDGEMENTS

I have many people to thank for helping make this book a success. First and foremost, I'm grateful to my husband Alex for encouraging me to write it when I described to him my conflicted feelings for the Church. Alex has been wonderfully supportive. He read multiple drafts, made suggestions, and cheered me up when I was feeling low. Without Alex, I doubt that I ever would have completed this manuscript.

I also wish to thank all the people in my life who showed me the true message of the Church with their faith and good works. The nuns who helped us as we were growing up, the neighbors and friends who were there when we needed them, the people I encountered during my 'prodigal years,' whose spirituality was real and whose beliefs were evident in their actions toward others, and the wonderful people of St. Sebastian's parish.

My family – my brothers, sisters, mother, and grandparents – helped shape my faith throughout my childhood. I'm grateful to them too for being there, for sharing my experiences and talking with me about theirs.

I also wish to acknowledge the managing editor of Fortuity Press, Steven Hamilton. His support throughout the publication process made what seemed at first an insurmountable task pain-free. His professionalism made my work easy.

There are so many other people who read drafts of various parts of the manuscript when it was being prepared, made helpful comments or encouraged me in other ways, that I cannot name them all. You know who you are, and I am extremely grateful to each and every one of you.

PREFACE

"According to current folklore, a young boy was once told about the many conquests of hunters over the lion. This story intrigued the little boy; he was puzzled and inquired, 'If the lion is supposed to be the king of the jungle, why is it that the hunter always wins?' The father responded, 'The hunter will always win until the lion writes his own story!'" (Shannon 1991:98).

* * *

Professor David Shannon tells this story in an essay published in 1991. Its wisdom is unmistakable. The victors, the oppressors, and the dominators always find a way to tell their own tales, to look good in them, and to be remembered. The 'lions' of the world, however, have no voices. Their opinions, their lives, and their struggles are unrecorded; their histories unwritten. Therefore, they will always lose.

This is the story of one lion – or, in my case, a lioness. In my 40+ years, I've maintained a conflicted relationship with the Catholic Church. A part of me loves it, is devoted to it. In some ways, I owe my education, my profession, my position in my community, even my marriage, to the Church that helped form my ideals and shape my conscience. In a real and tangible sense, I owe my life to the Church.

But another part of me feels distanced, unwanted, and excluded. The Church that helped educate me throughout my elementary, secondary, and post-secondary school years also taught me that men are superior to women, that women are unworthy of holding an ordained position in the holy Church, and that Blacks are inferior to Whites. It showed me the damage that racism and sexism can do to a person's self image. It had no patience for uncertainty, made no effort to help young minds resolve doubts. It compelled me to accept doctrine, tradition, and praxis unquestioningly. It discouraged me from seeking the truth. Finally, one day, the very Church that I so loved showed me the door.

Why I Left the Church tells of my formative years in the Church. My relationships with the nuns, priests, and my mother are remembered here as I reflect on incidents that sometimes brought me closer to God, sometimes confused me, and sometimes just plain frightened me. The image I have of myself as an adult, a woman, a parent, an African American, a teacher, a wife, and a scholar was shaped by the Church. The relationships I've developed with friends, colleagues, and fellow parishioners were molded by the many role models in the Church that I had as a child. In short, I am what I am today, in no small part, because of the Church.

So I struggle with this paradox: the same Church that has done great good for my family and me has also done harm in the name of God and Holy Scripture. Many priests and nuns found themselves caught in the evil web of racism. My own mother became both victim and victimizer as she tried to teach us that the racism we experienced at the hands of various priests and nuns was right and just. She was trapped, and tried unwittingly to hold us in the same trap. Lucky for us, time and persistence weakened the bonds of ignorance and we were able to escape.

Not everyone was so lucky.

PART ONE:

THE FORMATIVE YEARS

THE WEDDING

Winter 2005

It's always hard to turn left onto highway 46. Cars race across it all hours of the day and night. You might have to wait five minutes for a tiny opening. Since that was the way home from the post office, though, I tried to be patient. As I gazed into the oncoming traffic, I thought about the letter I'd just mailed.

Parish politics. Sometimes it's simply foolishness that, if you're smart, you ignore. Other times it hurts someone. This time, it hurt several people. And the worst part – the pastor was the major protagonist.

Normally when the political games start I look the other way. Who cares whether the collection money should be spent on a new refrigerator or a storage cabinet, or whether the new carpet should be gray or blue? But this time, a whole family was being hurt by our pastor's ego. It wasn't *just* Father George. But Father George had the power to put a stop to it, set a good example for the rest of the parish, and help out the Church in the process.

Instead, he took sides. And he sided with the ones who were doing harm. His actions were dividing our parish. So I wrote him a letter telling him how wrong I thought he'd been. I thought about cc'ing it to the bishop, but decided to wait and see how he responded first.

Not that I thought my letter would make any difference. After all, the politics only involved me indirectly, but Father George was setting a horrible precedent. He had been our pastor for only a little over a year, and if this was the way he was going to resolve problems – by taking sides without hearing the whole story and refusing to explain himself – well, we were all in for some trouble. I was incensed enough to consider leaving St. Sebastian's. I had searched long and hard for a parish where I could be comfortable, where a Black Catholic woman wouldn't be stared at or ignored, where I could take part in ministerial service of my own, interact with the youth of the parish, maybe even talk about some of the Black saints during Black History Month.

I'd been living in North Carolina for nearly three years before I found such a parish – little St. Sebastian's, only about 250 families. I'd been welcomed warmly to this community, and, for the first time in my adult life, I felt like I belonged. I'd grown to love this little community. But Father George's behavior brought back a truckload of memories – memories of events that forced me to leave the Church for a good part of my adult life. Maybe it was time to leave again, this time for good.

I pondered the possible consequences of the letter I'd mailed. Perhaps I'd be excluded from the few ministry programs that I enjoyed. Perhaps Father George would now shun me during Mass. Perhaps his supporters would begin behaving in ways toward my son and me that would make it impossible for us to stay.

Then again, my letter might make a difference. Maybe Father George would see how wrong he'd been and do the right thing, collect information, talk with both sides, apologize for his hasty decision.

Right.

No point in deluding myself – the only impact my letter could possibly have might be to make Father George try to think of ways either to garner my support or to hurt me. In all likelihood, Father George would simply toss my letter into the trash and forget about it.

And then, I thought back to the very first event that made me feel conflicted about the Church. It happened long before I was born.

* * *

Autumn 1957

"You may kiss the bride."

Roger and Beatrice are legally married. Two young adults – she is 20, and he is 21. But this isn't the wedding of Beatrice's dreams. It's a civil ceremony. A judge, not a priest, declares them man and wife. Since she was a small girl, Beatrice dreamed of a wedding in a Catholic church with a white dress, an organist, flowers, and a priest.

Beatrice had always been an obedient Catholic, a regular churchgoer. She attended Catholic schools all her life, even helped the nuns clean the church after hours. Roger wasn't Catholic, although he agreed to raise their children in the Church. He said he'd consider converting. But Beatrice's pastor refused to marry them. She and Roger asked again and again, but Father Charles absolutely refused. Why?

Because Beatrice is Black, and Roger is White.

To be fair, Father Charles eventually did sanctify their union – more than three years later, when they already had an infant son and another baby on the way. For the rest of her life, Beatrice lived with the guilt of having one child and conceiving another 'out of wedlock', according to the Church.

By 1957, the civil rights movement had begun. Brown vs. the Board of Education was already history. And the Church had yet to take a stance opposing the oppression of Black peoples.

* * *

Beatrice was my mother, and the child she was carrying when Father Charles finally blessed her union with Roger was me. She told me this story when I was about 10 years old. I don't remember exactly why she told me then, or what I said to her in response. But it stayed on my mind. The Church that my mother cherished so much in spite of its treatment of her, the Church that she insisted we love too – we made the nine 'first Fridays', we all wore scapulars, we prayed the rosary together – had let her down. Mom saw to it that we all attended Catholic schools, and missing Mass on Sunday was never an option. We would have to be practically at death's door before she allowed us to miss a Sunday or holy day. The fact that she was denied such a simple thing by her own pastor – a Catholic wedding – haunted me well into my adulthood.

That was the first time I had ever questioned the Church. Before then, the Church could do no wrong. The sisters and fathers were always right. Even their stories about the most unlikely of miracles couldn't be questioned. The nuns always knew what they were talking about. The priests were dispensers of grace and forgiveness, they were virtually infallible. Through them, and only through them, lay our path to salvation.

But suddenly, unexpectedly, they were flawed. How could a priest be a racist?

Over the years, Mom would insist that Father Charles was right, in a way. She and Dad separated six months after their fifth child was born. By then, Mom was pregnant with their sixth baby, but when she went into labor months later, the baby was breech. The doctor wouldn't perform a Caesarian section without Dad's consent, but Dad couldn't be found. They waited so long to decide what to do that Mom almost died that night. Finally, her father, my Grampa, convinced the doctor to let *him* sign the necessary papers. Mom lived, but my baby sister was stillborn.

A Catholic hospital, but no Catholic chaplain to comfort Mom, or to intercede on her behalf. Where was the Church then?

Mom believed, however, that the priest foresaw the divorce, which is forbidden. The 1950s was probably too soon for two people of different races to be joined in holy matrimony, she'd say. After all, being married to a White man *was* hard for her. They had trouble finding someone to rent them an apartment, he had trouble holding a job, they both had trouble with the neighbors, at the grocery store, at the park. The priest was right, she'd say.

But wouldn't a supportive priest have made it easier to bear the burdens of racism? Wouldn't the knowledge that their union was consecrated in the Church have given Mom, at least, more strength and confidence? If she'd had the support of her pastor and her parish, might they never have separated at all? Even when they did, wouldn't she have been better prepared to endure the trials she faced if she'd been more confident?

All my arguments were lost on Mom, but they stayed with me.

CONFIRMATION

"Like Baptism which it completes, Confirmation is given only once, for [both] imprint on the soul an indelible spiritual mark, the 'character,' which is the sign that Jesus Christ has marked a Christian with the seal of his Spirit by clothing him with power from on high so that he may be his witness" (Catechism 2006:para. 1304).

* * *

Winter 2002

I teach religious education classes (CCD) at St. Sebastian's. As soon as Martha, our Director of Religious Education, saw my parish information card – I'd indicated that I was interested in Ethnic and Educational ministry – she asked me to sit in on the CCD classes every Wednesday evening. After a while, she asked me to teach a sample class, and it went so well that she offered me my own class. I was to be in charge of the confirmation students.

For the next three years, therefore, I taught the 14- and 15-year-olds about the sacraments, miracles, the Ten

Commandments, the Bible, and the Creed. We engaged in role-playing exercises, created works of art with paints and glitter, and talked about faith and adulthood in the Catholic Church. St. Sebastian's doesn't have many children, but the few we have are bright, energetic, kind, and eager to please. And for three years, the candidates for confirmation of St. Sebastian's were the stars of the episcopal discussion periods. We received high praise from our bishop every year.

Every group of students I've taught knows my own confirmation story. I make sure that they understand that confirmation can be troubling for some children. If they're not ready, I tell them, they should wait. Waiting is nothing to be ashamed of. And if they want to talk to someone about their feelings of readiness, their conflicts, doubts, or fears, they can always come to me or to Martha.

I wish someone had told me that, all those years ago.

* * *

Autumn 1973

I was twelve, almost thirteen really. I would be thirteen by the time I received the sacrament. And my seventh-grade class was being prepared for confirmation. We had gone through our *Baltimore Catechism,* memorized the prayers, answered all the questions. "What is the purpose of man's existence? ... Man must know, love, and serve God in a supernatural manner to gain the happiness of heaven. ... Man cannot be perfectly happy in this world, for nothing created can satisfy his desire for complete happiness." Even at age twelve the use of *man* to indicate all humanity bothered me. That was just one problem with the *Catechism.*

The *Baltimore Catechism* strove to answer the questions that adolescent Catholics might ask. It did a pretty good job anticipating the questions. The answers, however, left a lot to be desired, at least by me. For seven years I'd been taught not to question the Church. We were to memorize and recite prayers, the names of saints, and lists of sins that violated the Ten Commandments. We had to be able to answer the various questions of the *Baltimore Catechism*. It was a dreary experience. We students were riddled with guilt for thoughts that we might be having. The nuns were often shocked by our questions – 'illegal' questions about sex or the seamier side of Church history.

By Spring, we were supposed to be thinking about our patron saints. We had to select a saint whose life had inspired us and choose that person's name. But I didn't have a saint. None of the saints had inspired me. Worse, the *Baltimore Catechism* hadn't taught me to be a good Catholic. It hadn't helped me see my place in the Church. It had done the exact opposite, shown me that there was no place in the Church for me.

I began to have doubts. Here I was, preparing for the greatest event of a young Catholic's life, and I wondered if the Church was for me. But the worst part of it all was the isolation. I couldn't talk with anyone – not my mother, the Catholic of Catholics, and certainly not the nuns. The nuns discouraged questions about Church policies, doctrines, or rules. Too many questions always brought the unsuspecting student frowns of disapproval, along with the occasional pitying shake of their be-wimpled heads. Questions for which the nuns had no answers were 'great mysteries', and only God could answer them. I was savvy enough at thirteen to know not to question too aggressively or to ask the wrong kinds of questions. We could ask about the mysteries as long as we didn't delve too deeply. And God forbid we express doubts about God's own Church.

Once, I asked Sister Patrice what I imagined was a cleverly-veiled question about my personal doubts. She saw right through me.

"Do you always have to go to confession before Confirmation?" I asked.

"Yes, dear, your soul must be very pure before the bishop anoints you with the sacred chrism", she responded.

"What would happen", I continued, "if you go through Confirmation and you're not sure you want to be confirmed? Is it a sin? How serious would it be?"

"WELL", the good sister continued, finger pointing at me, eyebrows raised, her gaze burning a hole in my soul, "it would be a VERY grave sin. Certainly a mortal sin. Your forehead might even burn where the sacred oil touched it! You must be very sure you're ready before you receive the sacrament."

Sister's answer gave me terrible nightmares. Night after night, I imagined myself in the line about to receive the sacrament, and when my turn came, my forehead started to burn. Or the bishop would know somehow that I was a sinner and refuse me the sacrament in front of my whole family. Or I would die immediately after the ceremony and go straight to hell because of the seriousness of the sin I had committed.

Deep down, I didn't *really* believe what Sister Patrice told me. How could the oil burn? And how could it be a mortal sin? Venial, maybe, but mortal? But years of hearing about those unlikeliest of miracles left a kernel of doubt in my mind. Maybe, just maybe, Sister knew what she was talking about. Maybe I should tell someone, have a heart-to-heart. But in whom could I confide? . . .

There was no one.

Soon thereafter, I came down with a horrible case of the flu. Fever, chills, stomach trouble – the works. And it kept coming back. Ten days of misery, followed by a day or two of relief, followed by another two weeks of misery. I missed a lot of school then, more than a month. And when my mother finally took me to the doctor, he couldn't find anything wrong. Maybe it was a relapse of the flu, he said. But the stomach trouble I described was so persistent, maybe, he thought, it was psychological. Maybe Mom should take me to a therapist.

Now, I had already lived for many years with my mother's mental illness. She'd been hospitalized multiple times with schizophrenia, and periodically suffered from delusions of being visited by angels or devils. So when the doctor said I might be suffering from a psychological illness – well, I would do anything not to have to endure the hell she was living. I did my best to put my problems behind me. I gave myself pep talks, I tried to forget about my doubts. Who cared whether I really believed? Surely I would learn to believe eventually, and if I didn't, so what? And my flu – or whatever it was – finally went away. I lost a lot of weight during that month, but I was probably a bit too heavy anyway. All would be fine. My mother chose my patron saint for me, since the sisters needed it during the worst part of my illness. And, God help me, I signed up to be confirmed.

Confirmation day arrived. I was terrified. What would happen? Would my sinful nature be revealed? Would my forehead burn? Would I go to hell? Would I embarrass my family?

At long last, the bishop called my name – my confirmation name, that is. He dipped his hand into the chrism, reached up, anointed my forehead and . . .

Nothing happened. No pain, no embarrassment, no hellfire. I had been holding my breath, was barely able to speak. The most vivid memory I have – my ONLY memory of that day – was the immense relief I felt when the chrism was applied and I didn't burst into flames.

* * *

Today, I wonder how much stronger my faith would be if, at age 13, I had been encouraged to probe the mysteries of Scripture. The sisters were almost afraid of questions. Did they think they would lose authority if they let us express doubts and explore them? Were they afraid we'd leave the Church? Or were they so accustomed to letting someone else do their thinking for them that it came naturally to them?

No matter the reason, this wasn't the first time I had endured sleepless nights because of the Church, and it wouldn't be the last.

ALTAR SERVER

"The Vatican issued a reprieve to altar girls in a document on the Mass published Friday, the draft of which raised the hackles of liberal Catholic cardinals and bishops when it proposed a ban on female servers at the Mass. [. . .] 'Girls or women can be admitted' to the altar for the Mass, according to a document published by the congregations for the Doctrine of the Faith and for Divine Worship and the Sacraments. The back down appears to be a victory for moderates over conservatives inside the Vatican, after the original draft, which said only boys could assist priests at the altar, was diluted after it was circulated to cardinals and bishops last year" (Agence 2004).

* * *

Summer 2004

Every Sunday we have to scramble to find an altar server at St. Sebastian's. Kirk was doing the job faithfully for many years, but when his father John fell out of favor with Father George, Kirk withdrew his name from the list of servers. We now have to rely on the older children –

Allen, Elaine, Brenda, or T.J. – and they're all pretty inexperienced. But if they arrive about fifteen minutes before Mass starts, one of them usually volunteers and struggles through the job. Even my own son Wesley has served a couple of times along with another child, but I won't let him serve alone until he knows the job better. I don't want him to embarrass himself by making a mistake. If none of the children arrives in time, however, Martha generally dons the alb and performs the task herself.

Today, girls can choose to become servers. The Church has begun permitting girls to serve God, their priest, and their parishes in this distinctive way. What a change from when I was a child! My inability to become a server in my youth when I had the desire had a huge impact on my young perceptions of my role within the Church.

* * *

1968

My older brother was an altar boy. Mom was so proud of him – Roger Jr. in his alb on the altar lighting the candles, helping the priest, ringing the bells and pouring the water, holding the paten under the chins of the communicants. Once or twice every month, from the time he was about nine years old until he was thirteen, we watched Roger serving on the altar. It was an honor for a boy to be selected as altar server. That's the way the role was marketed. All the altar boys had to memorize a series of prayers. Some were in Latin despite Vatican II. They also had to memorize all the priest's ritualized motions during regular Masses as well as the holy days and special occasions. The altar boys were supposed to learn to anticipate the priest's needs.

I remember Roger's altar boy handbook. It seemed long and thick to me at age seven, even though in reality it probably wasn't more than ten or eleven pages long. You'd have to be very smart to memorize that whole book, I thought. And Roger was an excellent altar boy. He anticipated the priest's needs every time and never made a mistake.

I was proud of Roger too. I tried to catch his eye at certain points during the Mass and smile at him or wink – it would have been a special status symbol for the altar boy to recognize his sister while in the service of the Mass! But Roger never acknowledged my smiles – either he was too wrapped up in his duties to notice me, or he was just that professional. Or maybe he didn't want his friends to see him smiling at his sister.

Roger was my hero when I was a child. He was my big brother, and until I was in college I wanted to be just like him – smart, brave, talented, and strong. And I wanted to be an altar boy like him too. I knew that there were no 'altar girls', but why couldn't I be the first? I pestered my poor mother for weeks. "Talk to the nuns," I pleaded. "Tell Father John that I could be an altar girl!" No one would have to know I was a girl – I would wear a hat so no one could see my braids! I would cut my hair! I could be just as good on that altar as Roger was. Give me a chance!

Mom, however, was unyielding. Altar girls were not allowed, and that was that. God never intended for girls to serve on the altar. If I wanted to serve God, I could be a nun when I grew up. But I absolutely couldn't be an altar girl. Finally her patient answers became threats – "One more word about being an altar girl and I'll tan your hide, girl!!" Time to give up on the dream.

I was resentful for a bit, but soon I forgot all about it. That booklet was awfully long, and it was nice just watching Roger from the sidelines. I got over my bitterness and life went on.

Years passed, and my baby brother Roland turned
ten. By then, Roger was 16 and getting too old to serve –
he was in high school and had lost interest in all that kid
stuff. And our parish had begun to shrink. Like so many
parishes in the 1970s, our neighborhood was suffering
from 'White flight', and the wealthier White parishioners
were moving out of the inner city and into the suburbs.
The poorer Black residents stayed behind, but many of
them weren't Catholic, and those who were didn't have the
resources of their wealthier White predecessors. Before I
entered high school our own parish merged with two
others, and we had to walk an additional mile to get to
Church. The population couldn't support three churches,
and the church and school nearest to us shut their doors,
creating a shortage of altar boys. For years, most of the
Masses were being celebrated without any server at all.
The priests had to learn to get along without help.

Roland dreamed of becoming a priest. After
graduating college he even entered a seminary for a year,
but then he realized that the priesthood wasn't for him. At
age ten, however, the lifestyle of a priest seemed
glamorous and wonderful. A housekeeper cleaned your
house and cooked your meals. The parishioners paid your
bills. And no heavy lifting! The priesthood represented
power and prestige, all in the service of God. We visited
the rectory a few times when the priests hosted receptions
for Christmas or Easter, and their home seemed like a
beautiful mansion to us. To have all that wealth and
prestige, all you had to do was say Mass a few times a
week, and you even got to change wine into Christ's blood
and bread into His flesh. Roland used to say imaginary
Masses in my bedroom when I wasn't there – he took a
missalette from our church and followed along with the
Sunday or weekday Masses. He went so far as to press
slices of bread into hosts. Mom even made him a child-

sized chasuble, green for the 'regular' season. I used to chase him out when I caught him, but he was never deterred, and I found him doing the same thing the very next week.

So when Roland turned ten, he started to wonder why there weren't any altar boys. Why couldn't *he* become one? He asked our pastor Father Vince about it, who agreed to give him a shot as long as Roger helped train him.

Six years had passed since I'd longed so to become an altar girl. It didn't faze me when Roland got the chance that I had been denied almost without trying – at least it didn't right away. The pages of prayers no longer had to be memorized, and it was no longer such a high-prestige job. Roger had had to train for weeks to get his chance on the altar six years beforehand, but Roland asked one week and found himself on the altar the next.

If there ever was a failure at altar boy, Roland was it. He was terrible! In all fairness, though, he'd received virtually no training. There were so few role models for excellence in altar service that he'd never seen it done well, except for when Roger served. And Roger hadn't been a regular server for a couple of years. But Roland hadn't listened to Roger's instructions, nor had he paid attention during all those imaginary Masses in my bedroom. When the time came to pour water over the priest's hands, Roland poured the water over the priest's shoes. When the bell was supposed to be rung at the transformation of the bread and wine, Roland forgot, and there was no bell. He was afraid to put the paten too close to the communicants, so if a sacred host were to fall, it would hit the dirty floor. Roland was the worst altar boy of all time. At least, he was the worst I had ever seen! And that was the last time Roland served on the altar.

Suddenly, I was fazed. I remembered my desire to be an altar girl. Why wasn't I given a chance? I was deprived of the opportunity because I was a girl. How could that be right?

* * *

2004. The year the Church finally relented. Altar girls were officially sanctioned by the Vatican.

It's a good sign, I suppose. Until then, altar service had traditionally been reserved for boys in hopes of encouraging priestly vocations. That's never been an option for girls. The Church isn't likely to reconsider its position in the near future, on the grounds that:

"Jesus Christ did not call any woman to become part of the Twelve. If he acted in this way, it was not in order to conform to the customs of his time, for his attitude towards women was quite different from that of his milieu, and he deliberately and courageously broke with it" (Women Priests 2006).

With girls on the altar, there may be hope yet for a real place for women in the Church.

UNLIKELY MIRACLES

"Miracles are signs of God's Providence over men, hence they are [. . .] simple and obvious in the forces at work, in the circumstances of their working, and in their aim and purpose" (Driscoll 2006).

* * *

February 2004

"St. Martin de Porres was a holy man." I begin my Black History Month lesson for St. Sebastian's youth. "All who met him could sense his kindness, his warmth, his compassion. He shared his food with the poor, even gave his bed to those sick and near death that he encountered in the city. Can you imagine? He would come back to his monastery with someone who had sores, or lice, or maybe even leprosy, and help him wash up, and let him sleep in his own bed. Often, the people he picked up would die in a matter of days. But they died with dignity. St. Martin de Porres gave them that gift."

"Yuck! Why'd he do that, Ms. Jean?" Haley, a young blond-haired CCD student, asks.

"Because respect for others is one of the most important tenets of the Church, Haley. It's a hard thing for us to remember when we're around people who are mean to us, or who maybe smell bad or are sick, or are just different. But we need to respect them and do what we can for them. We're all God's people. And we could find ourselves in their place some day, needing help from someone. We should treat people the way we would want to be treated."

Haley nods, and I continue. "Now, there's one more thing. St. Martin de Porres could perform miracles. He had the power of bilocation. That means he could be in two places at once. There are several reports of him being seen in two places far away from each other at exactly the same time."

"No way!" Spiky-haired Jake is skeptical.

"I know it's hard to believe, Jake, but the reports are very clear. He was in his monastery, with plenty of witnesses, and was reported on a whole separate continent by travelers who knew him. They had conversations with him. It wasn't just someone who looked like him. It was really him."

"How can you believe that, Ms. Jean?" Jake asks. "It CAN'T be true!"

"Faith."

* * *

Talk about unlikely miracles. Bilocation is a strange ability, but the reports about the various saints who possessed the power make it hard to dispute. Curing the sick, expelling demons, even raising the dead – somehow those are easier for children to accept than bilocation.

When I was a child, the nuns delighted in telling stories about the unlikeliest of miracles. Some were frightening. I don't know where they got these stories, but a few of them kept me up at night. When I was a child, I wondered sometimes if being a good Catholic meant having to endure nightmares.

* * *

December 1969

"Settle down, children! We'll do our Secret Santa in a just a little while. First, we have to finish our Religion lesson." Sister Mary Francis, a short, round nun with wire-rimmed glasses claps her hands to get the attention of her second grade class. A lock of bright red hair peeks out from under her wimple.

"I want to tell you a story about Saint Rowena of the Village. Rowena was born a long time ago – more than a hundred years! – in a tiny village. She could barely talk. She never learned to read or write. She couldn't add or subtract."

"She was retarded, wasn't she, Sister?" Dark-skinned Allen wears glasses and is a trifle overweight. He's a confident student, never afraid to ask questions.

"Yes, Allen, I suppose you could say she was retarded. But she was very holy. The only thing she ever learned to do was pray the rosary. And her favorite prayer was the Hail Mary."

"Couldn't she say 'Mommy' or 'Daddy', or 'I love you', Sister?" Light-skinned Rosie, her hair in pigtails and ribbons, asks.

"No, dear, she couldn't say anything at all except God's holy rosary. And she prayed it all the time. Day and night. Her little fingers grew bloody with all her praying."

Images of a child's bloody fingers flash into my eight-year-old mind as I gaze down at my own hand.

"No matter what fun there was to do – her brothers and sisters would play outside, running and jumping, laughing and catching butterflies – Rowena stayed inside, kneeling and praying until her knees grew bruised and bloody."

Knees too?

"Sister, doesn't God want us to laugh and have fun?"
I ask.

"Not when you should be praying, Jeanie! God
ALWAYS wants children to pray, all the time!" She lowers
her voice, which had grown a tad louder after my
question, and continues. "Now, little Rowena was a sickly
girl. She was weak and never had much strength. But
even when she was in bed, too weak to stand up or eat,
she had her rosary in her hand, and prayed the holy
rosary. Every ounce of her strength she devoted to it.

"Rowena grew weaker and weaker. Her Mommy and
Daddy prayed for her, they held the rosary in her hand for
her when she was too weak to hold it herself. And they all
– mother and father, sisters and brothers – knelt down
beside her bed every night to say the rosary with her.

"One morning, her mother came into her room and
there Rowena was, in her bed, the most beautiful
expression of peace and love on her dear little face, her
hands still clutching the rosary. She had died in the
middle of a 'Hail Mary'."

But the story isn't over yet.

"They buried her outside the church and her mother
visited her grave every day. One day, about six months
after Rowena died, she noticed a flower coming up from
where the little girl was buried. After a while, the flower,
which was the most beautiful tulip, opened up. And
inscribed in gold letters on its petals were the words of the
'Hail Mary.'"

Sister Mary Francis pauses while the children stare,
open-mouthed, at the unlikely story. She continues.

"The villagers wondered where the beautiful tulip
came from. So they tried to dig it up. They got shovels and
dug and dug, nearly six feet deep! At last, they came to the

source of the flower. The tulip's bulb was coming from the mouth of St. Rowena!

"Now, the moral of this story is that you should pray all the time. God loves the rosary, and you should say it whenever you can. Maybe God will reward you when you die like He did St. Rowena!" She smiles and claps her hands. "Now let's move the desks into a circle for Secret Santa!"

Somehow, I wasn't in the mood for Secret Santa after that story. I can't remember what my Secret Santa gave me. And I never felt quite the same about the rosary. The thought of having a holy tulip growing out of my mouth when I died didn't give me the comfort I'm sure Sister Mary Francis intended. Instead, it just gave me sleepless nights.

CONFESSION

Autumn 2005

This year, I only have three Confirmation students at St. Sebastian's, and only one is likely to receive the sacrament in May. The other two are only 12 and 13 years old, and our bishop prefers children to be at least 14 before receiving the sacrament. On the off chance that the bishop will change his mind, I'm teaching all three the same lessons. We've spent half the sessions so far on the sacraments.

It's strange that the students don't know that much about the sacraments yet. They know them by name – they recognize the names when they hear them, that is, but none could initially list all seven without help. They also couldn't explain what each sacrament represents, how they work, or why a Catholic goes through the process. We spent two whole class periods on the Eucharist.

This year, however, I discovered something disturbing at St. Sebastian's. Two of my confirmation students had never been exposed to the sacrament of Reconciliation, nor were they familiar with its more common name, Confession. I explained that Reconciliation is supposed to precede First Communion. They both had received First Communion, but somehow Reconciliation had been neglected. So this year I spent extra time explaining the rationale for Reconciliation, the process, and the benefits. Father James happened to overhear part of that lesson and volunteered that, traditionally, women have preferred to receive the sacrament in face-to-face, 'open' format, while men usually feel more comfortable in the confessional – the boxed-in closet that gives the illusion of anonymity.

None of the ignorance I saw this year is the students' fault, though, not entirely. We only meet for about an hour each week, and they don't have the same opportunity for practicing what they learn as I did when I was a child. When I was a little girl attending Catholic schools, we had Religion classes regularly. In the second and third grades, we studied Religion almost every day! And the nuns, of course, found a spiritual message in everything. We should go to daily Mass more often, they would say, if we earn a bad grade on an assignment, and God would enlighten us. We should pray more often if we have troubles at home. We should receive the Eucharist daily if we want to improve our reading skills and get A's. We said the Our Father and the Hail Mary every day, the sisters taught us liturgical songs, we heard stories about the saints during recess if the weather was bad outside. Talk about shaping eager young minds!

I was only about five years old when I first began to form ideas regarding Confession. One of my earliest memories of the Church, in fact, involves my mother's monthly treks to church. Mom used to go to Confession regularly. She'd get the five of us up a little earlier than usual on a Sunday morning and scoot us out of the house in time to arrive at church twenty minutes before Mass started so she could get a good place in the Confessional line. Roger and I used to watch the line inch slowly forward. The confessional mystified us – three cubicles joined together, the center cubicle for the priest flanked by ones for the sinners. Red and green lights flashed on and off as the repentant Catholics moved forward – green for 'Step Inside, This Cubicle is Open', red for 'Stop, Confession in Progress'. One-by-one, the ladies – they were almost always women – disappeared into the cubicles.

Neither of us understood Confession. We knew about sin – Mom taught us all about sinful souls, original sin, and the Ten Commandments as she was teaching us to read – so the fact that all humans are inherently sinful was something we could repeat almost verbatim to anyone who asked. The sisters loved that about us when we started school. Mom cautioned us to be still and quiet while she went to Confession, and we read our children's books or flipped though the missalette while she shuffled forward, hands clasped and head bowed in prayer.

Roger was always much more observant than I was. While we waited for Mom, he used to point out to me the irregularities in the tile pattern of the floor or show me new places where paint had chipped off the walls. He explained his imaginative versions of the meanings behind the stained glass windows and stations of the cross. I always believed him, no matter how fanciful his explanations were – nearly twenty months my elder, his age and sophistication bought him a great deal of credibility as far as I was concerned.

But neither Roger nor I paid much attention to the confessional until one particular Sunday when paint chips and stained glass somehow failed to hold our interest.

After careful observation, Roger figured out the mechanism and function of confession and explained his brilliant theory. The confessional, he observed, was like a time machine. Old ladies entered one of the cubicles, and emerged on the other side of the priest as young, beautiful girls, and vice versa. Our mother, of course, was the youngest, most beautiful lady in the line. So I was petrified – Mom may not have realized it, but she was about to be sucked into a time vortex! She would come out as a wrinkled old woman and die soon of old age, and we would be orphans!

Even now as I look back on that frightening incident, I wonder whether Roger was pulling my leg. He may have believed his story every bit as much as I did, but I don't know for sure. We both tried to warn Mom. We attempted to get her attention by waving and 'pssssst'ing' and pointing to the confessional. That got us several dark and threatening glares – not just from Mom either! – and a promise to make our bottoms sore if we didn't behave ourselves. So we stopped trying to warn her and tried to accept our fate calmly. I think I began to cry quietly to myself. It may have been the first time I prayed in desperation for a miracle. And sure enough, an old lady entered the cubicle on the other side of the confessional from Mom. We were doomed. But after a few minutes, our own beautiful young mother came out of the same cubicle she had entered. Our prayers were answered!

BANNINGS

"The Index of Prohibited Books, or simply 'Index,' is used in a restricted sense to signify the exact list or catalogue of books, the reading of which was once forbidden to Catholics by the highest ecclesiastical authority" (Hilgers 2006).

* * *

February 2005

Ash Wednesday. Since St. Sebastian's is so small, we have to share our priests with two other parishes in the area. Every year at this time, Martha tries to arrange for a priest or deacons to conduct a prayer service for us and distribute ashes. This year, Father James agrees to come. He's also agreed to hear confessions afterward.

Father James is St. Sebastian's most popular priest. Kind and generous, he's more giving of his time than any of our other priests. He even goes to lunch after Sunday Mass with the parishioners sometimes.

"Before I hear confessions, I want to go through the Ten Commandments, in case some of you've forgotten them. Sometimes even I can't keep track of 'em!" He chuckles a bit. "First, 'I am the Lord Thy God, Thou shall not have any other gods before Me.' No one ever breaks that rule so you don't have to worry about it.

"Next, 'Don't take the name of the Lord thy God in vain.' That one's about cursing. If you curse too much, you should try hard not to, and you can confess it tonight.

"Then, 'Keep holy the Sabbath.' If you miss Mass on Sunday, it's a sin. I'm not talking about if you're sick or have to take care of someone else who's sick, or if you have some kind of emergency or problem, or you can't get to Mass because your car breaks down and you can't get a ride. It's only a sin if you just don't WANT to go to Mass for no good reason.

"Then, there's the fourth one, 'Honor thy father and mother.' You kids, you should listen to your parents and obey them, don't talk back to 'em. That goes for your grandparents too, and your teachers. You should always respect your elders, especially your parents, who love you and do so much for you.

"The next one is 'Thou shalt not kill.' I don't guess any of you've killed anyone!" He laughs.

"Then there's number six, 'Thou shalt not commit adultery.' You all know what that one means.

"The next one is, 'Thou shalt not steal.' Don't go around robbing banks.

"Then there's 'Thou shalt not bear false witness.' That one's about lying. You shouldn't lie, it's a sin.

"The last two are 'Thou shalt not covet thy neighbor's wife or goods.' Try to be happy with what you have and don't always be wishing for what someone else has. It's not a sin to admire your neighbor's car or house and wish you had one like it, but it is if you start having bad thoughts, like wishing his new boat would sink or the brakes would go out in the new car, or something like that. That's when it crosses the threshold to sin.

"Ok, now there's a couple more things that aren't covered in the Ten Commandments that I want to talk to you about. Think back to whether you've read any books that the Church has banned, like *The DaVinci Code*, or ..."

Until now, I had been listening passively, enjoying Father James' humorous reflection on the Commandments. But my ears perk up when he mentioned the bannings. I hadn't read *The DaVinci Code* yet, but I'd planned to. And at that moment, I felt a flash of anger directed at Father James. How dare he tell me what I can and cannot read! How dare he, or anyone else for that matter, tell me what to think!

It wasn't really Father's fault. No doubt he was simply following instructions from some superior – maybe the bishop had sent out an announcement to the priests. Funny thing is, after reading *The DaVinci Code*, I couldn't find anything all that inflammatory about it. It's critical of the Church, but it's a work of fiction. More than 20 million copies have been sold worldwide. But some Catholics are so inflamed by what Brown has written that they've put a price on the poor man's head! (Newshog 2006).

Censorship offends me. Once authority figures in the Church, or our political leaders, start telling people what they can and cannot read, and once the people begin passively accepting it, we're no longer a free society. I'm not talking about responsible adults making sure their children don't get into pornography and violence. I'm referring to priests, bishops, and Church administrators telling grown people what they *must* avoid. The Church has every right to detail what it doesn't like about Brown's novel and to publish it in the form of a review, to circulate its review among the parishes, to elucidate the fact that it's a work of fiction. But it doesn't have the right to tell me, or any other adult, that if I pick up the book and read it I'm committing a sin in the eyes of God.

The irony is, *The DaVinci Code,* a work of fiction based on the premise that Jesus had a wife and child – what's so offensive about that? – is banned, but so many truly harmful media aren't. Consider, how much music, particularly rap and hip/hop music, advocates the use of illegal drugs, crime, savage violence, and misogyny? I have yet to hear the Church banning it, or even discouraging people from buying it.

Violent video games – games that feature graphic violence, killing, raping and/or maiming – have desensitized our children. In Florida recently, three men were convicted of beating six people to death over an X-Box (Word 2006). Yet I've never heard a single reference to a violent video game banning.

What about pornography, especially child pornography? In light of the recent pedophilia problems, you'd think it would be at the top of the banned list, but Father James didn't mention it. Maybe he thought it was covered under the sixth commandment.

And then there's the *Passion of Christ,* Mel Gibson's graphically-violent reflection of the last days of Jesus' life. It got rave reviews. For months on end, every Sunday Father George asked during his sermon how many of us had seen the film. He advocated it so strongly that he encouraged us to see it two, three times. "But bring some tissues, 'cause if you're like me you'll be crying your eyes out!" he'd say. "Every good Catholic NEEDS to see that movie!" Suggestion or command?

Such a violent film. My son Wesley was 10 years old when it came out. He begged us to let him see it, especially after Mass when Father had raved so much about it. But when Alex and I previewed it after Wesley had gone to bed one night, we had trouble getting through it. It was too violent, too graphically violent. How could we as parents forbid films, television shows, and video games for violence, and then advocate this?

How is it that so many of us can feel sympathy for Jesus, who was tortured and led to a grisly death, but not for the millions of African slaves, many of whom endured everything that Jesus did, even more in some cases? Not to minimize what Jesus had to go through – no doubt it was horribly painful and humiliating – but at least Jesus wasn't raped, at least he wasn't castrated or mutilated, not according to the New Testament. How is it that we can't feel sympathy for the people of Darfur who are being systematically exterminated in the name of 'ethnic cleansing'? Never in my life have I heard any priest, Black or White, lament slavery or genocide from the pulpit. What lesson have we really learned from Jesus if we refuse to apply it to the realities of our own lives?

* * *

Spring 1975

"Hey, whatcha doing over there?" Mr. Nelson, our next-door neighbor, walks over to the fence as I use the hoe to break up soil along our fence line. Our dog, Gilda, had run a path in our yard and I had just bought some grass seed to repair the damage.

"I'm getting ready to plant some grass, Mr. N."

"You sure are working hard, Jeanie. You're not supposed to work on a Sunday. It's God's day."

Mr. Nelson is Protestant – I never knew what faith tradition he espoused, they were all the same to us – and a part-time preacher at his local church. He's a nice man, a good neighbor, and has always been kind to us.

"I know Mr. N., but if I don't do it now I won't get a chance til next weekend, and I want it to start growing."

"Well, you still should rest on Sundays. Y'all been to church yet?"

"Yes sir, we went to Mass at 8:00. We've been home a long time." In fact, it's almost dinnertime.

"What'd you learn in church?" Mr. Nelson is always curious about our services. We've invited him to come along with us but he resists. He's invited us to his church too, but Mom says it's a sin to go to any church but a Catholic one.

"I don't remember, Mr. Nelson."

"You don't? Well, we talked about John, Jesus' little brother, and his relationship with Jesus and their mother Mary."

"Jesus didn't have a brother, Mr. N.! He was an only child!"

"No, he wasn't. He calls John his brother throughout the Gospels."

But Mary was a virgin. According to the priests and nuns, she stayed a virgin throughout her life, never soiling or cheapening herself with sexual relations. That's why she could be taken bodily into heaven. She was pure. How could she have had other children? Joseph would NEVER have had sex with her! But I couldn't say all that to Mr. Nelson. I decided to humor him instead.

"Really? I sure never heard that."

"Lemme get a New Testament, I'll show you." Mr. Nelson disappears into his house and returns a few moments later with some passages marked. He offers to let me read it for myself. I can return it in a day or so.

I finish my work, go inside the house and tell Mom about our conversation, showing her the New Testament that Mr. Nelson lent me.

"Put that away this instant, Jeanie! You shouldn't be reading it!"

"Why not, Mom?" I didn't understand her loud objections.

"Mr. Nelson is wrong! Mary was a virgin her whole life, Jesus had no brothers or sisters, and you shouldn't even be looking at the King James version of the Bible. It's a sin to have it at all! Put it down, and next time you go to confession you need to confess that you read it!"

At age 14, I was beginning to wonder why the adults in my life never seemed to have satisfactory answers to reasonable questions. What was wrong with the King James version of the Bible? Mom didn't know, but she was positive that we shouldn't have it. Father said so.

What if Mary really DID have other children? Why was that a problem? But my mother, the sisters and priests, and all my teachers, lay and religious alike, insisted that we believe unquestioningly. To ask questions was to sin. To seek the truth was to earn the disapproval of our elders.

THE ROSARY

2004

Two or three times every month, Father James celebrates Mass with us at St. Sebastian's. Father James is definitely 'old school'. He's 79 years old, and remembers the pre Vatican II days vividly. Every now and then he mentions the 'good old days' fondly in his homilies.

Everyone loves Father James. He always has a smile and a kind remark for everyone he meets. He makes time for us at the end of Mass for confession. He always takes one of the pastries that the ladies provide for the social hour after Mass and raves about how delicious it tastes – even when it didn't come out quite right. And he starts every homily with a joke. Usually the joke is a little stale, dated and old like he is, but we love them anyway. We laugh no matter how funny they may or may not be. Father James is a wonderful priest. He cares about us, he spends time with us, and we all wish he could be our pastor. Some of us think of him as our pastor in spite of Father George's official position. Father George has yet to convince us that he cares about the parish the way Father James does.

When Father James celebrates Mass, he comes early enough to lead us in the rosary. At about 9:40 everyone hushes, and Father begins. The children are scooted outside to play in the churchyard for 15 minutes so the rosary folks can have the quiet they need for peaceful meditation.

I rarely sit through the rosary at St. Sebastian's. Usually I'm engaged in some other activity – I greet the other parishioners as they come in, I watch the children, I talk with the other CCD teachers and plan the next lesson, I practice my reading if I'm serving as lector. But every now and again, I pick up one of the free plastic rosaries at the back of the church and join in. Unfortunately for me, however, the rosary has negative associations, and I rarely find peace or solace in the prayers. Praying those five decades of 'Hail Mary' sometimes dredges up old memories, feelings of discomfort and dread from my childhood.

* * *

1970

Every Wednesday for our first few years in Catholic elementary school – until the parishes merged – we children started our day at the church. Some Wednesdays we heard a quickie Mass – Father praying at the speed of sound, no homily, no special intentions, no socializing at the back of the church. In twenty-five minutes we were done and in our classrooms ready to learn. Other Wednesdays we knelt down in the church and prayed the rosary together. That took less time – we could be done with the rosary in fifteen minutes. All in all, our Wednesdays were barely affected. And the nuns were so happy on Wednesdays. They insisted that Mass or rosary was a great way to start a day. Maybe they were right – they seemed more relaxed afterwards even if we weren't.

The rosary. Four amazing mysteries – the Joyful. Glorious, Luminous, and Sorrowful. Each mystery serves as a focal point for meditation. The faithful meditate on the five decades – ten Hail Marys per decade – and try to come to a deeper understanding of the meaning of Jesus and Mary in our lives. The Luminous Mysteries are new. Introduced just a few years ago by Pope John Paul II, the Luminous Mysteries remind us of the ways that Jesus revealed himself to us as God.

The rosary can be a wonderful meditation. I have a good many friends who use the rosary to relax in heavy traffic, or find comfort praying it after a difficult day at work. It only takes a little time, and you can gain insight on your place in the world and in your community. You can find solace. You can become more sensitive to the ways God reveals his great presence to us.

So why was it stressful for us as children? . . . The Sorrowful Mysteries. Almost every time we said the rosary as children – said, not prayed – we contemplated the Sorrowful Mysteries. The Agony in the Garden, Scourging at the Pillar, Crown of Thorns, Carrying the Cross, and the Crucifixion and Death. Five bloody, agonizing, gruesome events in the life of Christ. Mom, the sisters, and the priests seemed to want us to focus on the most painful events in Jesus' life.

I dreaded the rosary. A fifteen-minute-long reminder of pain and agony that I had personally inflicted on poor Jesus with my sins. As a child, fifteen minutes seemed a lifetime to me. A lifetime to consider the pain that Jesus endured for the sins of the world – specifically, of course, my own sins. The white lie I had told, the time I hit my brother, the unkind words I had for my sister – for all these failings of mine, Jesus had been tortured, eventually dragged to a particularly gruesome death. All because of me. It was horrifying.

The guilt that the Sorrowful Mysteries instilled in me didn't last long enough to make me perfect and flawless. After saying the rosary, I still hit my brother from time to time, I still yelled at my sister, I even disobeyed my mother occasionally. And I had to endure the guilt of all my childhood failings – those failings that had resulted in Jesus' miserable death for my own personal sins. The Sorrowful Mysteries instilled just enough guilt to terrify, but not enough to change.

Mom believed that old cliché – the family that prays together stays together. About once a week, Mom summoned us, sometimes cajoling, sometimes threatening, and we knelt down in the living room as she announced the intention of the rosary. For her, every rosary was prayed for the intention of reuniting her with our estranged father. If we prayed hard enough, she believed our father would leave his new family and return to us. It never happened, but until the day he died my mother believed it would.

Maybe the Sorrowful Mysteries were an appropriate meditation for Mom's unrealistic hope. Perhaps my mother envisioned herself suffering as Jesus had. Maybe her own feelings of betrayal resonated with Jesus' betrayal by Judas and the apostles. And I know she could relate to the grim consequences of the betrayal – she had suffered more than the rest of us when my father abandoned us. But no experience in my childhood allowed me to relate to Jesus' suffering.

The Sorrowful Mysteries were frightening, and the nuns elaborated on each mystery to ensure that we understood Jesus' pain. The Agony in the Garden – anticipation of the betrayal and horrible death he was about to endure so agonized Jesus that he began to sweat blood. The Scourging at the Pillar – the whip literally tore the flesh from Jesus' back. The soldiers put the crown of thorns on his head and dressed him as a king, and when they took the robe off him, it must have been like being whipped all over again. The nuns, it seemed, had contemplated Jesus' suffering and death and had a keen understanding of what he went through. They wanted to share it with us. And every time we sinned, we were scourging Jesus all over again.

* * *

As a mother, I understand that a little guilt isn't always a bad thing. Heaven knows that I've tried to guilt my son Wesley into behaving himself. It works sometimes – the imagery of a hard-working teacher who goes out of her way to make his school experience pleasant and fun, and the hurt she must feel when he backtalks and insults her can bring tears to Wesley's eyes. It can keep him out of trouble for at least a day or two! But I haven't tried to make Wesley bear the personal burden for all the things that Jesus suffered. Sure, I've told him that it hurts Jesus when he lies or otherwise misbehaves. But we don't spend hour upon hour dwelling on it.

When I was a child, all the pain that Jesus endured was described to me in graphic detail. I was told about hellfire and how horrible it must feel – how hell must be an eternity of torture. I burned myself once when I was six. Mom was ironing clothes and when she turned her back I started playing with the iron. And I remembered how much it hurt. It must have been something like the pain of hell fire. I was told how God watches me all the time, that He sees me whenever I do something wrong or sinful. I don't, however, remember many discussions of the goodness and joy that God can bring to our lives. I don't remember being told that God loves us no matter what. I have no doubt that my mother and the nuns said those good things to us, but the imagery of the Sorrowful Mysteries and hellfire drowned it all out.

SEX

"In Christianity [. . .], the image of women that has emerged over the centuries has been dualistic, upholding women as the 'font of purity,' as exemplified by the Virgin Mary, and at the same time stigmatizing her as the 'source of all evil' as evidenced by Eve's seduction of Adam" (Hayes 1998:103).

* * *

Summer 1968

Our cat Boots had just delivered a litter of kittens in the living room closet. Five tiny, furry, wiggly little life forms crawling around in the cardboard box we'd found. I had witnessed the last two emerging from the womb into the world. That image opened up a whole world of curiosity about birth. My mother could barely handle the constant barrage of questions.

"How did Boots know she was gonna be a Mommy?" I ask.

"All mommies just know. When the time comes they go to a quiet place where the babies can be born."

"How did the babies get into Boots?"

"God puts a seed of life into the mommy's womb. The seeds grow and grow, and when they're ready, they come out."

"Does that mean if I swallow an apple seed I'll be a mommy too? Maybe I'll have a baby tomorrow!" I chatter excitedly, having eaten an apple earlier in the day. I knew I'd probably swallowed a seed! When my new baby arrived, I would call her Sally.

"No, Jeanie, that's not how it works. It has to be a special seed. Only God can put it there."

Oh. "How come the babies came out of Boots' behind?"

"What? They don't come from there. What makes you think that?" My mother was confused. Maybe she didn't know.

"'Cause I saw it! They came out of her behind! It was the same place where Boots goes for number two!" I was unshakable in my certainty.

"No, Sweetie, they didn't come out of Boots' behind, they came out of her worst place." 'The worst place' was our term for genitalia – vaginas and penises.

My eyes opened wide. The worst place! The place God hated most of all! How could cute, cuddly, loveable kittens come out of such a foul, sinful place?

Scandal! Surely Mom didn't know what she was talking about. No beautiful baby – human or feline – could come from *the worst place*. . . . But Mom seemed so sure.

"Mommy, why does a baby come from the worst place? I thought they popped out of the belly button!"

Poor Mom. No doubt thinking that now was the time for 'the talk', she decided to tell me the whole story.

"Well, Jeanie, here's how it works. When a Mommy and a Daddy fall in love, they try to have a baby. They take off all their clothes, and then the Daddy puts his worst place on the Mommy's worst place, and then, a few months later, they have a baby, and it comes out of the Mommy's worst place!"

. . . Oh my God! Total shock – I have a hazy memory of myself staggering out of the room half terrified, wondering vaguely how dark a room would have to be for two naked people to touch each other's worst places with their own worst places. No room in the world could possibly be dark enough! I don't think I said a word for several days, horrified by the miracle of conception and birth.

* * *

After having five children, you'd think my mother would have a healthier attitude toward sex. But no. At least as far as her five children were concerned, sex and everything associated with it was dirty.

Mom's views about sex were influenced by what the nuns and priests taught. On the rare occasions we talked about sex at home, invariably Mom explained that Mary was pure, clean, and close to God. She never soiled herself with worldly desires or nasty habits with men. She was perfect, untainted, and sinless. And to my mother, 'sinless' translated into 'virgin.'

Mom was an only child, and told us many times how lonely she had been growing up, how she'd wished for a brother or sister. That's why she wanted such a large family. If she and Dad had stayed married, she would have kept trying to have children. She hoped for at least 10 babies. And, as she undoubtedly understood, you can't have babies without sex. All pleasure in the sex act aside, just the thought that you needed it for children demonstrated that there was something good about it. To my mother, though, sex was a dirty little private ritual you had to go through in order to get what you wanted, like going to the bathroom to get relief, or gutting a cow to get a tasty hamburger. Dirty, foul, and not to be discussed in polite company. She passed her views onto all five of us. It's no wonder that only two of us ever married.

Even when we entered adolescence, Mom had very little to say about sex. When we turned ten, each of the three girls got a booklet about 'becoming a woman' that purported to explain the menstrual process, albeit in the most confusing of terms. They had virtually nothing to say about sex, however.

I remember once during Lent, all six of us – Mom and we five children – were sitting around the kitchen table looking over a handout one of us had gotten explaining the Ten Commandments. Mom wanted us to talk about them together as a family. Below each Commandment was a list of actions – or thoughts – that violated it. Under number six, the handout specified that oral sex, anal sex, and masturbation were forbidden, but not one of us kids had the faintest idea what the terms meant. We turned to Mom.

"Well, oral sex is . . . it's when . . . well, . . . " She turned red, got up, walked to her bedroom, and closed the door. We had to wait until the following day and look up the definitions in the huge dictionary in the school library.

* * *

Spring 1979

Senior year. St. Mary of the Woods Girls' Preparatory School requires four years of religious education. Senior year was meant to include sex education so that the young women would know what to expect from their husbands when they got married.

The sisters realized that they were ill-prepared to teach young girls what they needed to know about sex, so they hired a lay person – a <u>married</u> lay person, so as to avoid any misunderstanding – to teach the girls about sex.

Mrs. LaRue, Catholic, married five years, had all the answers.

At age 17, all I knew about sex was what I had read in the dictionary. My all-girls high school prevented me from meeting any boys who might 'educate' me, and, in the process, leave me with a little bundle of joy to raise on my own. Most of my classmates managed to meet and date boys anyway, but I didn't. The only boys I knew aside from my brothers were guys I'd met during my summer jobs, and Mom didn't allow any of the girls to date until college.

Mom was strict, and at the time I resented my lack of freedom. But when a few of my classmates ended up leaving school before graduating – one friend had a baby at age 16 – I grudgingly accepted that maybe my mother was right. At any rate, I was so much of a nerd that I actually preferred working on interesting school projects to going to dances and such. Flinging myself around in skimpy, provocative clothing to gain the perverted attentions of some filthy, ignorant boy – my mother's words – didn't really appeal to me. So by senior year, I was the only one in my class who had never been on a date. At least I was the only one who admitted it.

Many, perhaps most of my classmates, however, were sexually active, and I knew it, although I avoided any discussion of sex. My mother considered those girls 'bad'. My grandmother would have called them strumpets and trollops. I remember one high school scandal. A classmate left school in the junior year, and when we all returned in the Fall, we learned that she had posed nude for some men's magazine. Everyone, students and teachers alike, whispered about it for weeks.

I was expected to think of my sexually active classmates as bad influences, as wayward oddballs. I never did, though. They were misguided, lacking in self-discipline, perhaps hedonistic, but they were my friends and peers. *I* was the oddball.

I sure wasn't ready for Mrs. LaRue. Not a modest bone in her body! She talked about the menstrual process out loud in the classroom. She told us when she was on her period and having cramps. She lead a discussion on the advantages of tampons over feminine napkins. Once, she asked one of the students at the beginning of class if she could borrow a tampon! Outrageous!

I'll never forget the way she described losing her own virginity.

"Let me tell you about my wedding night, girls. I was a virgin – never even came close to having sex! There was so much to do before the wedding – getting my hair done, making sure the food and the flowers were right, visiting with all my family and friends." She shows us pictures from her wedding album. "I was exhausted at the end of the day! By the time Mike and I got to our hotel room that night, we were both too tired for sex! We just flopped onto the bed and went right to sleep."

I imagine two attractive twenty-year-olds hanging half-on and half-off of their individual twin beds. It never occurred to me that they would've been in the same bed.

Mrs. LaRue continues. "So the next day, I knew something was wrong with me! I mean, how can you be a virgin the day *after* your wedding? I was so embarrassed, you wouldn't believe!! Can you imagine?"

No, I couldn't.

"So the next day, I was under so much pressure! I had to have sex or else there really would be something wrong with me. But I was nervous! I was tight as a corkscrew! When we finally had intercourse, it was so painful! It wasn't the least bit pleasant! Talk about a bad memory . . ."

Sex hurt? How could it? As far as I knew, you just touched your worst places together. I was a naïve 17-year old.

"It took some time, but eventually sex became very satisfying for me. You want to know what made it good? Love. You have to learn to love your mate in that special way, and then, it becomes natural to want to please him."

Shock! Horror! By now I was surely beet red, wondering whether I should turn away or pretend to listen.

"You know what makes premarital sex a sin? It's not some man placing his penis into your vagina, it's..."

That's all I heard. The imagery of a penis going into a vagina was so seductively terrifying that I didn't hear the end – the climax, so to speak – of the story. I suspect, however, that she said something about love and commitment.

* * *

What a strange woman to find in a Catholic girls' school. I have to admit, however, that I learned a lot from Mrs. LaRue, as scandalized as I was at the time by her frank talk. She was the first adult in my life to talk about sex like it was a normal thing to do, not a dirty little secret that good people with strong moral fiber avoid, that people HAD TO do when they got married, and that only weak, nasty sociopaths enjoyed.

IMANGES

"*Saints of Africa number in the thousands. They include three popes, three Doctors of the Church, eight Fathers of the Church, thousands of martyrs, hundreds of monks, plus countless religious and lay leaders. Africa possesses a rich heritage in the annals of Christian heroes and heroines whom the Church selects as saints. Yet, who among readers in the Western Hemisphere can name more than a few of these saints?*" (O'Malley 2001:11).

* * *

Winter 1974

"Mom, where'd you get that picture?" Mom had tacked to her bedroom wall an 8 x 10 image of Jesus, his head and shoulders only. He had the requisite halo, but otherwise this picture was far different from any I had seen.

Jesus had shoulder-length, slightly wavy, dark blond hair, professionally styled and neatly parted in the center. He had perfectly chiseled features. His beard and mustache were impeccably groomed. His nose was straight, proportioned and shaped as the handsomest Northern European movie stars. His eyes were a light, hazel brown, almost golden with fine arched eyebrows. His lips were a delicately sculpted mauve, turned up oh-so-slightly into the faintest of smiles in an expression of peace. His skin was milky white, just a tiny shade darker than his pure white clothing and with the barest hint of pinkish coloring on his prominent cheekbones. The Jesus of this picture was the handsomest man I had ever seen, at least according to 1970s Western aesthetic standards. I was completely absorbed.

I gazed at the picture, half in love with the man who was supposed to represent my celibate god, as my mother answered. "One of the missions sent it to me. I mail them donations and they send me pictures and things."

"Can I have it?" I couldn't take my eyes off of it.

"No."

"C'mon, Mom! That's the best Jesus picture I've ever seen! Let me have it!" My teenage love would not be denied.

"No, Jeanie, it's mine. You can't have it."

Was Mom as struck by the image as I was? Had she fallen in love too?

"Can I borrow it then? For a week?"

"No. You'll just have to send your own money to the missions and hope they mail you one!"

And that was that. It didn't occur to me until years later that that picture didn't look the least little bit like either of us. From the light skin, to the yellow hair, to the straight nose, Jesus was as different from us as day is from night.

* * *

It's no coincidence that today, a picture of Jesus often resembles the people for whom the image was painted – White with straight brown hair for White people, darker skinned with thicker hair for Hispanic peoples, darker still with thick curly or kinky hair for Blacks. But when I was a child, all the pictures of Jesus I ever saw represented him as a White man. Sometimes he had brown hair, sometimes blond, but always his features were European. For us, Jesus was White. It was a White man's world, after all. The nuns said that frequently during class. Just like David Shannon's story about the hunters and the lion, Jesus was, and is, depicted as White because Whites, or people indoctrinated by Whites, are telling the story.

One day, when as I was teaching a sophomore level Great Books class, I challenged some of my students' images of God. They assured me that no one cared what Jesus looked like, that the symbolism mattered far more than what the image looked like. So I bought a poster of an African Jesus – dark skin, thick lips, dark, piercing almond eyes and thick curly hair – and hung it in a prominent place in my office. The Black students smiled when they saw it. Some of the White students did too. But most of the Whites became visibly uncomfortable, trying to avoid my eyes and putting their backs to the poster. Some turned red. A few started to stutter as they talked to me. Apparently, it DID matter what Jesus looked like.

Does Jesus' physical appearance make any difference to us at all? Surely the historic Jesus looked like a young Semitic man. But whether our images of Jesus are Black, White, Jew, Hispanic, or Asian, it's his message that means something to us, not his appearance. It shouldn't even matter whether Jesus is represented as a man or a woman. But don't say that to a Catholic.

INTELLECTUAL FREEDOM

"Catholics, when compared to Protestants, still have a great unfamiliarity with the Bible; this is a result of the type of narrow and paternalistic thinking of the last [19th] century, as characterized by the passage (from the Dogmatic Catechism's English translation in 1871):

"'The Church forbids that the Bible [...] should be given to be read by all persons indifferently. [...] The proof that it cannot be a good thing to put the Bible into the hands of all persons is, that being full of mysteries, it would injure rather than profit the ignorant'" (Conwill 1998:204).

* * *

Autumn 1980

Dr. Eugene Rosenthal, Professor of Theology at the University, begins his lecture.

"The Pentateuch covers the first five books of the Old Testament: Genesis, Exodus, Leviticus, Numbers, and Deuteronomy. In Jewish tradition, these five books are called the 'Torah'. Make sure you read them if you haven't already.

"Let's talk about their authorship. There are four sources for the Pentateuch – the Yahwist, the Elohist, the Priestly, and the Deuteronomic authors, or traditions, or strands. . . ."

What?!? There are *sources* for the Bible? Sources aside from God??? And our professor wants us to *read* the Old Testament?

Dr. Rosenthal continues. "And think about the passages I've listed on the blackboard. I want you to write a reflection of the passages' relevance in their historical context, and what they mean to you personally."

Wow!

All my life, catechism class consisted of reading and memorizing lists of sins, prayers, and saints. We had to read our missalettes, catechism books, and whatever else the sisters thought necessary to nurture our souls. We were told what to think and how to feel. But we were never asked to read from the Bible. I wasn't even sure we had a Bible in our home.

And heaven forbid we bring up the authorship of the Bible! Aside from the four evangelists and Paul, it was considered virtually heretical to suggest any author aside from God.

Dr. Rosenthal opened my mind to a whole new world of questioning, probing, analyzing, and uncovering meaning in the Bible for myself rather than relying on other people, maybe not as well educated as I was, to read and interpret it for me. We discussed the Bible as one document among many and talked about it in its own historical context. We talked about the non-Biblical references to the life of Jesus, the social history behind His actions and their impact on His world. We read the Psalms as poetry, not as lists of instructions and warnings.

I absolutely loved the class. Dr. Rosenthal knew Greek and Hebrew. Every now and then he would write a passage on the board in the original language and discuss the nuances in meaning. Dr. Rosenthal and his syllabus were a breath of fresh air for me! What a vivid contrast to my high school and elementary school religious education.

* * *

Winter 1976

"Mom, do you believe in Adam and Eve?" I ask. During catechism class that day Sister Mary Thomas had spent a long time on the story, how Eve had been responsible for the fall of all mankind, how they realized after the fall that they were naked and therefore sinful, how nakedness itself was a sin.

"Yes, I believe the story." Mom responds. "Why?"

"But do you believe it literally – do you think there really was a Garden of Eden, and that Adam and Eve lived in it and that God threw 'em out?"

"It's in the Bible, Jeanie. It has to be true."

"But what about the people Cain meets after he kills Abel? Where did they come from? And what about Noah and the Ark? How could Noah build a boat so big that he could fit *all* the animals in it? What about all the insects? The microscopic creatures that he couldn't see? And what about animals that didn't live in his part of the world, like polar bears? He'd have to make a boat the size of Detroit! Or even all of Michigan! He couldn't do that!" The same questions that most every Christian asks at some point.

"Why do you think you know more about the Bible and Church history than the priests and nuns do, Jeanie? You're 15 years old. There are a *lot* of things you can't possibly know or understand."

"I'm not saying I know better, Mom, I just want to talk about it. If it's true, why is it so hard to believe? Is it a sin if we don't believe?"

Mom was stumped by my question. Was it a sin or not?

"What do the nuns say?" she eventually responds, somewhat bewildered.

"I've never asked them." I was afraid to. It would be obvious by my question that I doubted the literal truth of the Bible. I didn't want to incur their wrath if they thought my doubts were a sin, I didn't want them to dislike me, and I certainly didn't want to get an F in religion class. How do you shut that door once you've opened it?

"I guess what I really want to know is what the big deal is," I tried to explain. "What if Adam and Eve is just a story, like the parables Jesus told? Maybe God wants us to think about how good it would be if we trusted Him completely, and how bad it is when we have doubts and go against his word. Besides, what difference could it possibly make if Adam and Eve really existed, or if they didn't? Isn't the message more important than whether the story is really true?"

Mom thought about what I'd said for a few seconds. She nodded, like maybe she'd had that same thought herself when she was my age. Perhaps she agreed with me. But it was too much too soon. After a quick moment, she shook herself out of it.

"I think the Bible was written by God for us to understand how to live our lives, Jeanie. And God doesn't lie to us. Maybe it wouldn't matter whether Adam and Eve lived or not, but they did, because it's in the Bible. I'm gonna believe it. It's the job of the priests and nuns to help us understand, and to tell us what to believe, so we don't have to be burdened with doubt. I DO believe in Adam and Eve and the Garden of Eden, and Noah, and everything else. You should too. Stop questioning things you can't understand and accept what the nuns tell you to!"

So ended my first attempt at an honest, rational discussion of the Bible with my mother. Frustrating as it felt at the time, maybe we had made some headway.

* * *

Since I became an adolescent, it's bothered me that our teachers, the priests, and the nuns felt they had to act as our intellectual filter. I can't remember ever being asked during catechism class, 'What do YOU think?' We students, we parishioners, were told what to think at every turn. Most Christian denominations refer to the Old and New Testament explicitly. Most good Christians have their own Bibles and bring a copy to church with them. But not Catholics. The Church, in its infinite wisdom, has decided what sections of what Old Testament and New Testament passages we should think about every Sunday and presents it to us in the missalette. After all, our pope is infallible, at least he is when he speaks *ex cathedra*.

That cloak of infallibility, however, filters down into Catholic popular culture to include not just the cardinals and bishops, but the priests and nuns too. What a burden it must be. What a powerful aphrodisiac, to be considered infallible by hundreds, thousands, maybe millions of people. How much harm has been done in its name?

ST. JUDE

January 2005

My husband Alex and I have been married for nearly 20 years. Since we announced our engagement, my mother has been after me to try get him to convert to Catholicism, but I've never taken her seriously. Alex and I get along as well as we do *because* we respect each other's beliefs. For the most part, we share the same ideas about morality, ethics, goodness, the nature of sin, and what happens to us after we die. But Alex was raised in the Methodist faith. There are some aspects of Catholicism – particularly some of the traditions – that he can't quite wrap his mind around. Some things he finds downright amusing.

"I just don't get the saints thing. Why do you pray to saints? We Methodists pray straight to God. We don't need any intermediaries! It's almost like you have a bunch of little gods and one big one!" Alex says with a laugh.

"It's not like that at all, Hon! We have saints to remind us of all the good qualities that human beings have. We're reminded of all the love, compassion, courage, and strength that we can find in ourselves with faith. And the saints aren't like little gods – they're more like God's pals, and since they're in heaven they already have God's ear. The saints are God's agents!" I laugh a little myself. "Seriously, we don't really pray TO saints. We pray to God *through* the saints."

"What about St. Jude? Isn't that the saint your Mom is always praying to? Patron saint of impossible cases? Seems to me a saint like Jude keeps people like your mother from getting on with life."

"Yeah, but no one really believes that St. Jude can do the impossible. It's Catholic popular culture."

"Then why do you have a little St. Jude statue on your computer monitor?" Alex questions.

"It was a gift from my mother!" I respond defensively as I glance protectively toward the statue.

* * *

Prayer to St. Anthony, patron saint of lost things:

"Tony, Tony, turn around. Something's lost that must be found." And when you've found what you're looking for: "Tony, Tony, turn around. Something lost has now been found!"

When you want to sell your home, bury a statue of St. Joseph upside down in your front yard and it'll sell right away.

Why do we believe these things? Thousands, maybe millions of Catholics hold these beliefs that the Church doesn't really endorse. But the common folk swear by them. And then there's St. Jude.

I've never been able to find anything to substantiate the legend of St. Jude. There doesn't seem to be any real link to the idea that his intercession can fix impossible situations. But don't tell that to people like my mother.

* * *

Spring 1972

"Mom, why do you have a picture of St. Jude on the wall?" At age 11, I'd just started to question my place in the church. I'd started wanting explanations for the practices, proof for the beliefs that my mother and the nuns espouse. I would eventually have to learn to censor myself.

"Because St. Jude is the patron saint of the impossible." Mom explains.

"What do you want that's impossible?"

"I want your father to come back to me – I want St. Jude to help me reconcile with him."

We had recently learned that my estranged father had remarried and was starting a family with his young bride. Ten years my mother's junior, she was already pregnant with their first child. I didn't realize it then, but it must have been a terrible blow to Mom. Personally, I didn't much care. I hadn't seen my father for seven years. As far as I was concerned, he was out of our lives for good. We got along fine without him.

"Why do you want him back, Mom? He's got another wife now. We don't need him!"

"Jeanie! You take that back this instant! Your father and I are still married in the eyes of God and the Church, no matter what he does with that little tramp! He's MY husband! And we DO need him! You children need a father!"

Yikes!

"Sorry Mom. But I don't see how St. Jude can help. What good can he do anyway?"

"He's God's most powerful saint, and can cure diseases that no doctor can cure, and can solve problems that no other saint can handle. We can always turn to St. Jude when no other saint comes through for us. And I pray to St. Jude every day that your father will come back to me! You should pray to him too. You should pray that your father comes back to you!"

Not understanding my mother's passion for St. Jude, and worrying about the possibility of schizophrenic relapse, I made whatever promises she seemed to want to hear and beat a hasty retreat.

Nearly every day, my mother prayed for Dad's return. She insisted that we children pray too – she had us pray the rosary together, she made us promise to make novenas, she lit candles and paid to have Masses said for his speedy return. Until the day he died 30 years later, she prayed to St. Jude for reconciliation. About 15 years ago she added 'winning the lottery' to her short list of impossible intentions. But Dad never returned, and, to this day, she hasn't won the lottery.

* * *

Alex is right, I think. My mother was forced to live without my father, but because of St. Jude she never put aside the hope that he would return. After all, St. Jude *would* make it happen, it was only a matter of time. She believed that as firmly as she believed the sun would rise tomorrow. So she never really got on with her life. My mother was an attractive woman, but because of her belief in St. Jude, she never talked with another man, not even just to pass the time. She never made new friends, male or female, never attempted to develop a new skill, start a new career or a hobby. She wouldn't read a book unless it was about one of the saints. She was always too busy preparing for Dad's return. She wouldn't have time for friends or hobbies or careers once he came back.

I can't really put the blame on the Church for my mother's short-sightedness. Maybe it's a case of faith-gone-wrong. After all, the nuns also preached 'God helps those who help themselves.' My mother interpreted that saying to mean she should pray more.

What about my own little St. Jude statue? I've never believed the hype about St. Jude, but there he stands, atop my monitor. How many times have I tried to throw him away? I actually tossed the statue into the trash the last time we moved, not knowing where to pack it and wanting him out of my life. But 10 minutes later, I snuck back into the kitchen and fished him out. I washed him off and stashed him in my purse.

Strange.

THE SERMON

"At present there are four recognized ways of treating the homily [...]:

"The first method consists in treating separately each sentence of the Gospel. This was the uniform method of St. Anselm, as we gather from the sixteen sermons that have come down to us. It is not to be recommended, for it gives, at best, but a fragmentary and scattered treatment.

"The second method is quite the opposite; it focuses the entire content of the Gospel in a single idea. It is usually called the 'higher homily'[...].

"The third kind selects some virtue or vice arising out of the Gospel, and treats one or the other to the exclusion of all else. This kind of homily is commonly called a 'prone'.

"The fourth kind is that which first paraphrases and explains the entire Gospel, and then makes an application of it. This, the method of St. Chrysostom seems, except where the 'higher homily' applies, to be the best [...]" (Beecher 2006).

A homily, therefore, is expected always to expand on the Gospel in some way. But not every homily I've heard follows these guidelines.

* * *

October 2004

Sunday. Today's Gospel reading is from Mark – the story of the rich young man who wanted to follow Jesus but couldn't give up his wealth. I've always liked that story – how far are you willing to go for your beliefs? A good story about choices and convictions.

But young Father George doesn't see it that way. He never mentions the story at all during the sermon. Instead, he uses the homily as an opportunity to espouse his personal political views. His disarming Southern style allows him to deliver a politically charged message that goes barely noticed by most of the congregation.

"Election day is coming up! How many of you are planning to vote?" A show of hands – just about every adult in the church. Father continues. "It's great to live in a democracy, isn't it? We get to choose our own leaders.

"Everything we do, you know, should reflect our faith. When we get up in the morning, say our prayers, dress for work – what about those women who dress so provocatively? You can see everything! Nothing left to the imagination, am I right? And all the makeup, and the plastic surgery to make some things bigger and some things smaller – isn't vanity a sin? Those women don't have any self-respect, do they?"

My head begins to ache as Father's misogyny creeps out – again.

"But as I was saying, our faith should be reflected in the way we vote too. How could a Catholic vote for someone who supports abortion? That's wrong, isn't it? Killing innocent little babies is definitely wrong! Some of our political leaders support abortion, even some Catholic ones!" He shakes his head mournfully. "They'd better wake up and smell the coffee, people! Hell is a big place, filled with people who kill babies!

"And what about 'gay rights'? God created Adam and Eve, not Adam and *Steve*! Am I right?"

Father's been reading homophobic bumper-stickers again. He continues.

"Now, I'm not saying that God hates gay people. God loves everyone, right? That's what we're all taught in catechism. But God wants us to live together as man and wife, a man and a WOMAN! Two men or two women together? That's just unnatural! So we absolutely can't support gay marriage, can we? *Can* we? God definitely objects to THAT! Matrimony is one of God's sacraments, and we have to protect the holy institution of marriage! Am I right?"

What does gay marriage have to do with the readings? The Catholic Church is free to uphold a ban on gay marriage within its ranks if it so chooses – already does, in fact. No one is questioning or threatening that right. And how does one protect the institution of marriage by preventing gays and lesbians from marrying? What's the threat?

"What about that judge who wants to keep the Ten Commandments outside his courthouse? How can a good Catholic possibly object to that? And they're gonna force him to take them down or he'll be fired? They keep saying, 'what about the rights of atheists or non-Christians'? Why should we care about the rights of people who hate God? What about OUR rights? What about *GOD's* rights? We Catholics should be offended when they DON'T display the Ten Commandments! Doesn't God want us to remember them? Don't the Ten Commandments BELONG in a courtroom? Don't they remind us of what's right and what's wrong? But these crazy liberals, they say, 'separation of Church and State!' Why, I ask? Shouldn't we think about God whenever we create a new law? Church and State shouldn't be separated, they should work together, right? Wouldn't THAT be a wonderful world!"

Isn't that the way it works in the Taliban? Religiously sanctioned torture and ritual rapes/murders, stonings, all in the name of someone's interpretation of the word of God. I guess Father George forgot that little tidbit. But the sermon isn't over yet.

"We also have to pray for our troops. They're taking the ultimate risk for us, aren't they? They're fighting terrorists so we can keep our freedom. It takes a brave man to order our young men to defend us. So we need to pray for our president too. Pray that God continues to bless him, and support him, and guide him."

Has Father forgotten that this was a pre-emptive strike against people who had not threatened us in any way? An unjust war. Even the pope has condemned it. Our freedom isn't at stake. Why is Father supporting it?

"We should also remember that God LOVES America. Doesn't your heart feel warm whenever you see those bumper-stickers, 'God Bless America'? And we've got to defend it against people who want to take away all our liberties. Not just the liberals, but the terrorists. God wants us to love our enemies, so we've got to pray for them. Yes, I know, no one WANTS to pray for Osama Bin Ladin. As good Catholics, though, we really have to. We can pray that Jesus will show Osama Bin Ladin the light. But that doesn't mean that we support terrorism.

"In the name of the Father, and of the Son, and of the Holy Spirit, Amen."

* * *

My head is reeling. Political propaganda, misogyny, and homophobia, all in a single morning. He might as well have been flying a banner, "Vote Republican if you're Catholic!" Sure, he's entitled to his own – albeit misguided – point of view. He can tell anyone he wants how he plans to vote during the social hour. But spouting political propaganda from the pulpit, giving a special kind of legitimacy for his personal viewpoints? An irresponsible action if ever there was one.

This wasn't the first time I'd heard priests using the pulpit for a political platform. In fact, it was fairly common in my experience. I wondered why Father George wasn't worried about losing the parish's tax-exempt status. More importantly, why wasn't he interested in the message of the Gospel and the readings? The personal affront to those of us who don't share his personal convictions is secondary to the failure of our priest to lead us in a reflection on the message of the Word.

As I try to shake off the headache that Father George's propaganda caused, my mind wanders back to my mother and the things the priests and nuns had *her* believe.

* * *

Autumn 1998

Every Saturday morning I telephone my mother. She lives alone now, and looks forward to the regular conversations with her children. It's the highlight of her week.

"Tell me about the neighborhood you're living in, Jean." Mom asks. I'd accepted a job at a local college and have just moved into a new house.

"It's a mixed neighborhood, Mom. Blacks, Whites, and Hispanics live here. I like it. It's kind of loud though. Lots of kids play in the street after school, sometimes well into the night. I don't mind it too much, but Alex really hates the noise."

"Who's making the most noise, the Black kids or the White ones?"

"I don't know – probably about the same, I guess. Why?"

"It's probably the Black kids. Their parents don't teach them to behave."

Not THAT again! My mother is always putting down Black people. A special kind of self-hatred.

"Mom, you've never seen my neighborhood and you assume that the Black kids are the worst. And let me tell you, there's this one kid, a White kid, *definitely* the worst kid on the block, always causing fights, calling other kids names. The Black kids are no worse than those White ones, and maybe even a little BETTER-behaved!"

"That's probably because the Black kids provoke the White ones."

Always defending the racist view. "Black kids are no better and no worse than the White ones, or the Hispanic or Asian ones, Mom. They're all just kids."

Mom has an answer prepared, though. "That's not true, Jean. Remember the curse of Ham? All Black people bear the stain of Ham's disobedience."

The curse of Ham?

"The priests always said so – I've heard that lots of times, haven't you?" Mom responds. "The sisters and priests tell that story every so often. It's true. Father even said it a few weeks ago during the sermon."

I'd heard that interpretation, but had dismissed it. I don't put much stock in the racist ramblings of some ill-informed or malicious priest or nun. But then again, I was born in a different generation.

I try to get her to see reason. "What about the fact that God made all of us in His image? God loves all of us equally? God created us equal? Men and women, Black and White – we all have the same potential for good and bad choices."

"But God has to punish people for doing bad things, Jean. That's why we had so many centuries of slavery – God was punishing us. That's why God made Black people uglier than White people, with thick lips and nappy hair. It's a reminder of the curse."

How can she believe that?

"But I do believe it. I don't see how you can disbelieve it! That's what the sisters told me in school, and what the priests said during Mass. They wouldn't lie to us. That's why White people are so much smarter than Black people. I don't know why you wanted to live in a mixed neighborhood anyway. Alex is White, and you're light-skinned. Why didn't you want to buy a house in a White neighborhood? *I* sure would have! Black people don't know how to keep their houses clean, or their yards, and their kids mostly turn to crime and drugs. You lock your doors at night, don't you?"

Such contempt!

"How could you *think* such terrible things, Mom?!? You're talking about your own people!"

"Because they're true! White people are cleaner and smarter, they have better things and they know how to take care of them. Black people are lazy and kind of slow. Their brainpans are smaller than White people's. We learned that in school. They've done all kinds of experiments. But I don't hold it against them! Black people can't help being inferior. It's God's truth. The nuns and priests told us."

The curse of Ham. How many priests and nuns, perhaps in genuine desire to teach and explain the apparent injustice of racism, have relied on the curse of Ham as evidence of God's will?

And what if the curse of Ham never existed? At least, not in the way that we Black Catholics have been lead to believe?

* * *

"[The] development of the dualistic perception of women during the period of slavery in the United States [...] placed White women firmly in the role of upholder of purity and Black women in the role of dehumanized temptress. These polarized definitions became firmly embodied in American society, continuing today in the almost universal depictions of Black women as 'welfare queens' and single mothers, while White women are more often seen as the feminine role models of society. This dichotomous way of viewing women became a part of the self-understanding of many in both the African American and European communities" (Hayes 1998:103).

* * *

July 1977

Summer months were always hectic in our parish back home. The regular priests often took their vacations then and spent time with their families. Some weeks, we had to scramble to find a priest for Sunday Mass.

This week, old Father Grayson has the pulpit. He's a retired priest, close to 90 years old, but still feisty and opinionated. He's old enough to have gone to school in the generation or two following the Civil War. His sermons leave no doubt where his sympathies lay.

Today's sermon is from Paul's letter to the Ephesians. His 10-minute ramble-fest is too long AND too opinionated for my tastes.

"Paul says, 'Slaves, obey your masters in everything, not only when you're being watched but in simplicity of heart, fearing the Lord.' He says the same thing in Colossians! What does it mean? I know we don't have slaves anymore, but we're all slaves to God, don't you see?

In the olden days, slavery wasn't always so bad. Slaves were part of the family. When Paul was alive, slaves were like children, and the masters took care of them, like God takes care of all of us. A lot of 'em couldn't take care of themselves! And everyone got along with everyone else. Not like today! You just look at someone funny and all of a sudden you're prejudiced! What's this bunk about Civil Rights? We were all happy! We got along. Nobody was trying to get out of his place, getting uppity and rising above his station!

"Now, like I was saying. This passage is a lot like his letter to Philemon. Philemon's slave ran away, and the slave – his name was Onesimus – Paul sends him back to Philemon. Why would he do that if he thought slavery were wrong? Because it was only wrong if they got mistreated! Everyone's a slave to someone else! If you got a job, you work for your boss – you're a wage slave. And you women, your husbands are masters of the household so that makes you their slave. Paul says that too – 'Women be submissive to your husbands!' And we all work for God. Who needs Civil Rights? Or Women's Rights? We should be worried about serving God, not some stupid equal pay and integrating schools, all that miscegenating around! We respected each other! We had a Negress for a maid when I was a boy, she was our nanny, and we loved her like part of the family. She had four head of children, and we all played together. She was respectful! And we took good care of her too. We gave her our old clothes, some of 'em like new! And we gave her extra food, and paid her real good. It was like Paul said, we treated her justly and we got along fine! Nowadays, there's no respect anymore! You can't get a Negress to clean your house, they're too good for it! They'd rather be on welfare! And the men, they're all militant; it's no wonder most of 'em are in prison!

"So you should remember what Paul said. Be good to your bosses, trust 'em, and they'll take care of you. And don't go trying to be better than God made you!"

Thank God the church was mostly empty for this early morning Mass.

* * *

After Mass as the six of us walk home together, Father's ramblings are still stirring around in my head. I tried to talk with Mom about it.

"What'd you think of that priest, Mom?"

"He was ok."

"You don't think he was prejudiced?"

"No, Jeanie. He wasn't being prejudiced. He was just telling the truth."

The TRUTH!?

The real truth is, *we* were on welfare – Aid to Dependent Children (ADC) – because Mom couldn't hold a job, and we all felt guilty about it. Funny looks at the check-out line when we took out our food stamps to pay for our groceries, at the doctor's office when we pulled out our green card. Why do people always blame the victim? Mom's second hospitalization pretty much sealed our fate. She couldn't handle much pressure anymore, and since Dad had skipped out on us and never bothered to pay child support or alimony, we would've starved without help from the government. Yet WE were the ones made to feel guilty, not our ne'er-do-well deadbeat Dad. And my mother's childhood years of being told that Blacks were less intelligent, lazier, and morally inferior to Whites were no longer just a nasty myth. In her mind, they came to fruition the day she signed up for ADC. The word became flesh, so to speak. She was the last person to challenge the stereotypes. As far as she was concerned, she WAS inferior. Inferior, miscegenating, and lazy. Poor woman.

You hear something from your role models often enough, you begin to believe it.

* * *

Now, almost 30 years later, my 60+-year-old mother still believes the same racist propaganda that she was fed as a child. I never knew how deeply she had internalized it until now. No wonder she's schizophrenic. It's a miracle that every Black Catholic of her generation isn't institutionalized.

What if Paul had never written those famous words, "Slaves be obedient to your masters"? How might our experience as Black Catholics have been different, perhaps better, if we'd never been forced to hear those words over and over again?

TRANSUBSTANTIATION

Transubstantiation – the belief that separates good Catholics from Protestants. Jesus himself is present, physically present, in the bread and wine on the altar. The host and the cup of wine aren't merely symbols of Jesus, they ARE Jesus. And when we take communion, we are consuming Jesus' body and blood.

So why does it taste like bread and wine?

The great mystery.

I believe in transubstantiation. I didn't always. When I was a teenager, I – like the kids I teach in CCD class – thought it was just a silly story. I spent hours as a child staring at the priest during the Eucharistic prayer.

"This is my body, which has been given up for you." The bell rings.

But no matter where I'm sitting, I could never see that circle of unleavened bread change in any way at all. It looked like a circle of cardboard, it tasted like cardboard. How could it be the body of Jesus Christ? It takes a great deal of faith to believe. Maybe you have to be an adult before it begins to make some kind of sense – or before you decide to accept it in the face of all evidence to the contrary.

* * *

Autumn 1971

Round-faced, perky Sister Mary Peter tries to encourage the children to attend Mass every Sunday. Mass alone, however, is not enough. The fifth graders need to take communion as well.

"What's so very important about Holy Communion, children?

"'Cause Jesus is in the communion, Sister!" Reddish-brown skinned Donna, her hair in pigtails, responds.

"Good, Donna! You've been paying attention. Now, why is it good that Jesus is in the communion? Jimmy?"

"'Cause even though Jesus is dead we can still be with him in the communion." Curly haired with a honey-brown complexion, Jimmy is always eager to participate in discussions but never quite gets it right. Sister is surprised, but controls her initial reaction and removes her hand from her mouth.

"Oh, no Jimmy! Jesus isn't dead. He rose again, remember? He's with us all the time."

"Even now?" Jimmy asks, looking around the room.

Sister smiles. "That's right, Jimmy, even now. Especially now! Let's talk some more about communion. Why is it so good that Jesus is in the communion? Beth?"

"How do you know that he's in the communion, Sister? It still looks like a wafer when you take it." Dark brown skin, her hair made up into a little afro with a headband around it, Beth is skeptical.

"Because that's what our faith tells us. Jesus himself told us that at the Last Supper! But it's very important that we take Holy Communion every time we get a chance. Every day if possible! Why?"

The class is silent. No one can fathom what Sister is trying to get us to say.

"Because the Church tells us to?" Jimmy tries again.

"Because our parents make us?" Jerome asks.

"Because it makes us holy?" I finally get through to Sister.

"Exactly right Jeanie! Exactly right! Now, HOW does it make us holy?"

Silence again. Sister Mary Peter's mind is inscrutable. What in the world was she getting at?

"Children, surely you've heard the expression, 'you are what you eat'. Can't you apply that here? Jeanie? You know the answer, don't you?"

" . . . Because . . . when we take communion every day, we become . . . Jesus?"

Could that be it? Could it be the answer?

"YES! Finally! You've got it, Jeanie!" Sister Mary Peter beams, and continues on with the lesson.

But now I'm confused. Taking communion turns us into Jesus? Is that true?

* * *

As a child, Sister Mary Peter's imagery stuck in my mind for a long time. I should take communion as often as possible, maybe even several times a day? The more I took, the more I would look like, smell like, think like Jesus?

But I didn't want that. I wanted to be myself. I wanted to look like myself, think like myself, and not be haunted or possessed. I thought about the people with the demons from the New Testament. Would it be better to be possessed by Jesus? Or was any possession, any loss of free will, a tragic thing?

In my fifth-grade mind, I reasoned that perhaps I should avoid communion if I cherished my identity. I wanted to love Jesus, but be myself. Although I couldn't have said it this way back then, I cherished my free will. But how could I avoid communion? If everyone in the family gets up to receive communion on Sunday except me, what would my mother think?

How much of myself would I have to give up by continuing to practice Catholicism?

WHITE FLIGHT

"The assumption of the statistical insignificance of Black Catholics in the U.S. Catholic population is seldom challenged or analyzed. Most Roman Catholic dioceses and parishes do not have or use a regular systematic, standardized, and objective method of gathering ethnic-cultural statistics. Yet statistics are often used to legitimate closing Catholic institutions in predominantly black geographic areas. One reason given for the closing of Catholic schools and churches in the inner city is the fact that most of the population in the community and schools are non-Catholic; yet in the past these schools and churches have been the base for the church's evangelizing efforts among African Americans" (Phelps 1997:29).

* * *

Autumn 1974

"Open your Math books, chil'ren. Everybody work on chapter four. Write out the problems and solutions to the odd numbered ones." Mrs. Ryan turns to Marcus and me. "Jean and Marc, you two work on your algebra books."

A middle aged Black woman, Mrs. Ryan had a way about her that reminded us all of our favorite aunts. Somewhat matronly, she smiled easily, sometimes brought candy or cookies to school, rarely scolded us, never reported anyone for disruptive behavior. Yet, somehow she managed to keep order in a classroom filled with about thirty-five 14-year-olds that, simply because of who we were, scared just about all our other teachers. We were all incredibly fond of her. Too bad she didn't know how to challenge our minds.

"What problems do you want us to do, Mrs. Ryan?" Marcus asks. Tall, skinny, awkward, brown-skinned, wearing horn-rimmed glasses, Marcus is the brightest boy in our eighth-grade class. I'm the brightest girl.

"Oh, whatever y'all want. You can work together. Slide your desks on over."

"Ok. We'll work on chapter three." I respond. We open our books and work in a corner of the room, where we can access the blackboard.

After a few minutes, Marcus and I both realize we're in over our heads. "Do you understand this one, Jean? How're we supposed to solve for x?" We're both confused, and call for help. "Mrs. Ryan, would you help us for a minute? We can't get this one." I show her the example in the textbook, the work we've tried to do, and the wrong answer that we keep getting.

"Honey, I don't know how to do THAT! I never was any good at math. Y'all just gonna have to skip that one and go on to the next one." Mrs. Ryan chuckles a little and walks over to another group that's doing something less complicated. Marcus and I continue to work. Eventually, we begin to get it. At least, our answer matches the answer in the back of the book. But we realize that we're on our own. As far as eighth-grade Math goes, we're entirely 'self-taught'.

* * *

"African American urban neighborhoods are seen by both insiders and outsiders as places of drug-related crime and violence dominated by fear. Outsiders consider most Blacks to be a group of lazy and dependent persons who lack moral integrity and intellectual capacity. Many are unprepared to relate to African Americans in other than their stereotyped image of Blacks as poor, violent, criminal elements within society." (Phelps 1998:71).

* * *

May 1975

"Okay kids, you all should've started thinking about what classes you'll be taking next year in high school by now." Mrs. Elrod, a small, high-strung White woman that the students generally dislike, was our English teacher. Most of our classes were taught by the homeroom teacher, Mrs. Ryan, but Mrs. Elrod came to our class every day for an hour to review the basics of grammar and writing. One day, she decided to have a 'heart-to-heart' with us. "How many of you are planning to take a foreign language?"

About three quarters of the class raise their hands. She continues. "Who's gonna take Spanish?" A few hands go up. "What about French?" A few more. "Who all wants to take Latin?"

I'm the only one planning to take Latin in ninth grade. My grandmother had taken me to orientation and signed me up. I was looking forward to it.

"Well, I'd recommend you forget about Latin. It's way too hard. You should all take Spanish. It's the easiest language. You can handle THAT language. Now let's go over yesterday's worksheet."

Condescending bitch.

. . . I didn't realize how bitter I still felt about Mrs. Elrod's patronizing comment until I started writing this story decades later. You'd think I'd have let it go by now.

But back then, that's why we all hated her. She didn't like us, didn't believe in us, didn't take time to encourage us, hardly ever had a good thing to say about our work. A young White woman stuck in a predominantly Black Catholic school. She probably thought, like most people, that there weren't enough Black Catholics in the entire nation to fill an elementary school classroom. The few she might encounter would be irrelevant. Instead, nearly all of us were Black. And we were still irrelevant.

* * *

We went through four teachers in eighth grade. Except for Mrs. Ryan, all were White. The three White ones didn't last. Sad thing is, they probably would have been good enough teachers in a 'traditional' Catholic school. But to be in charge of a room filled with 29 Black kids and only four or five White ones – that was too much for them. They were anxious, unsure of themselves, maybe even a little afraid of us.

First, there was nervous, thirty-something Mr. Donaldson. The boys intimidated him. Most were Black, but the few White ones scared him too. He was fine with the girls – tentative and uncertain, but not frightened. One day, he had a breakdown in class. Just started stuttering, gasping for breath, and crying. We never knew exactly what caused it. It happened out of the blue. That was the last we saw of Mr. Donaldson.

Then there was Mr. Samuels. Mr. Samuels – a young White man - was almost blind. Short, skinny as a rail, with stringy brown hair, bad skin, and thick, thick glasses, Mr. Samuels envisioned himself the hippest teacher of all time. He used hip lingo, wore platform shoes and plaid pants, and told us 'Funky Fairy Tales' – his own creation – between classes. Dreary things, neither interesting nor clever. He tried to be our friend. Wanted us to accept him as a peer. But he too was intimidated by the boys, Blacks and Whites alike. He actually got into a fistfight with some students. One day, he walked into a glass door. Some of the kids started laughing, and Mr. Samuels threatened them. Simon, one of the White boys, kept laughing after everyone else stopped. Mr. Samuels got up in his face, shouted at him, and pushed him. Simon – taller than Mr. Samuels by a head – pushed back. It escalated. Jerome, one of the Black kids, tried to break it up. He stepped in the middle and held Simon, saying, "Let it go, Man! He's a teacher!" But Mr. Samuels attacked Jerome, grabbing him and shouting something about being able to handle himself. He threw Jerome into a locker and punched him. Another male teacher eventually broke it up. And that was the last we saw of Mr. Samuels.

Then there was Mr. Wertner. He couldn't handle the pressure. He was a tall, blond, attractive young White man. Most of the girls fell in love with him during those three weeks he was with us. But he was insecure as hell. Couldn't stand it when someone corrected him, but wasn't smart enough to get things right all the time. He broke down one day when trying to explain DNA. Someone – Marc – asked what the initials DNA stood for. But Mr. Wertner didn't know. "Deocto- . . . Deoctoribosome . . ."

Foolishly, I chimed in. "Deoxyribonucleic Acid, Mr. Wertner." Normally I listened quietly as my teachers said whatever they wanted, right or wrong. To do otherwise was disrespectful. This time, though, I just couldn't stand it.

"No, Jeanie, that's not it. It's Deoctoribosome Nu . . ."

"Naw, Mr. Wertner, Jeanie know what she talkin' about!" That was Grady. He spoke up for me a lot – I think he had a crush. I give Grady a tiny, tentative smile.

"Jeanie doesn't know THIS, Grady! Let's just see. I'll look it up in this book." But lo and behold, I was right.

Poor Mr. Wertner couldn't take the shame. Every day for the three weeks he was with us someone asked him a question he couldn't answer. Mr. Wertner was young and inexperienced. No one really expected him to know everything. If only he'd been a little less self-conscious. He needed to learn to say 'I don't know, let's look it up together.' But Mr. Wertner couldn't stand to be wrong in front of so many Black students. Not every day. It went against everything he thought he knew about Blacks. Maybe it would have been different if we had been White. Maybe he could have taken it a little better. We'll never know for sure. So that day, he walked out of the classroom. That was the last we saw of Mr. Wertner. And after Mr. Wertner left us, Mrs. Ryan took over for the rest of the year.

Three White people, all young, all trying to make a difference. They'd passed up the higher salaries they could surely have earned in a public school to do something they thought they believed in – teaching in a Catholic elementary school where religion was still part of the curriculum, where students prayed every day, where teachers were taken seriously and respected. But none of them – not a single one – had any experience dealing with Black people. We scared them. We intimidated them. We made them feel insecure. The only person who could handle us was a poorly prepared, undereducated Black woman who treated us with kindness and respect and didn't feel threatened.

Funny thing was, we weren't all that bad. No serious behavior problems at all. No one brought drugs or weapons to school. No one threatened the teachers. We didn't even use profanity. We were teenagers who sometimes were loud, and sometimes had bad attitudes. That was it. But we scared the bejesus out of three people who weren't ready for a room full of Black adolescents.

* * *

White flight. Integration of middle-class neighborhoods during the late 60s and early 70s resulted in hordes of Whites fleeing to the suburbs. Lower-income-earning Black families couldn't afford to finance their parishes and schools as well as their White predecessors. So schools and churches closed. Parishes had to merge.

Every year, there were fewer Whites in our neighborhood. When we moved into our home in 1971, the neighborhood was about half White and half Black. Three or four years later, all the Whites were gone. White-owned businesses left too, and there were fewer opportunities for Blacks to make money. Low incomes kept Black families living 'on the edge', and homes began to fall into disrepair. Poverty and crime went up as housing values went down. It was pretty dismal. My brothers and sisters and I attended three schools in three years: Holy Family, St. Benedict, and St. Luke/St. Joseph. Each one closed its doors at the end of the year. By the time I entered eighth grade, the nuns were gone as well. There wasn't a single sister at St. Luke/St. Joseph Elementary. Just a few priests to teach us catechism. We were left with teachers who either didn't care about us, actively disliked us, and/or were incompetent.

How *should* the Church have responded to White flight? The priests couldn't very well force people to stay once they'd decided to leave. They couldn't try to drive Blacks away from the White neighborhoods – though a few priests did try. John McGreevy documents a great many incidents in New York City, Philadelphia, Chicago, Boston, and Detroit in which priests actively encouraged their parishioners to resist the integration of their white neighborhoods, stirring many of them to violence (McGreevy 1996).

I wonder, though, how much effort dioceses expended on providing well-trained Black teachers for the schools that were losing their White students. Or, how much sensitivity training they could have provided for the White teachers who were committed to staying.

Insecurity about the closing schools and the teachers' condescension and lack of faith in us marked the later years of my elementary school education. Those years could just have easily been marked by excitement and enthusiasm about learning. If only our teachers had tried to like us. Instead, we were stuck with Mrs. Ryan, who couldn't solve a simple math problem and had trouble with grammar and pronunciation. But I'll take a Mrs. Ryan any day over the Mrs. Elrods and Mr. Wertners. At least she gave us room to learn on our own. At least she respected us.

PART TWO:

LEAVING

THE DOORS CLOSE

Winter 2005

We always take great care at St. Sebastian's not to ignore the visitors. We try to take a moment to acknowledge them, smile and say "Hello, welcome, and please stay for some cookies after Mass." We try especially hard if the newcomers are different in some way – if they're elderly, or don't speak English very well, or are members of minority groups. We want them to feel welcomed, and we want them to come back.

It was St. Sebastian's warm welcome that coaxed me into joining the parish. Twenty years ago, however, I was virtually showed the door of parishes I visited. It was the last straw.

* * *

Autumn 1983

College graduation had finally come and gone, and I'd packed my bags for graduate school. Four years in one of the nation's Catholic colleges had helped reaffirm my faith in some ways, but also managed to keep me naïve about the world. Even through college, certain questions about the church were considered 'illegal', with the priests becoming defensive and uncomfortable whenever they were raised. Best to avoid those topics and get on with life.

My graduate school, however, was located more than 500 miles from home, the farthest I'd ever been from my family. I was unsure of myself. How well could I survive on my own? My mother, still receiving welfare since her schizophrenia prevented her from holding a job, wouldn't be able to help me. My small stipend wouldn't go very far, and I was expected to send money home whenever I could. I didn't know anyone in my new town, didn't know how much to budget for utilities. Heaven forbid I have an emergency. I didn't dare consider getting a car – far too expensive and unpredictable – and relied on my one-speed bike and the Greyhound buses for transportation. I didn't have a telephone, scared that long-distance bills would clean out my meager savings. I longed for the comfort and security of a church community, and sought out a parish as soon as I got settled into my tiny one-bedroom apartment. As luck would have it, there was a Catholic church just a couple blocks from my place. I started attending Mass.

At first, I sat in the back of the church and observed. Were the people friendly? Did they laugh and talk with each other, or did they come to Mass and leave right away? Was the priest kind and compassionate? Did he visit with the parishioners?

Weeks passed, and I realized that the people didn't seem to enjoy Mass. They went to church and left. Five minutes after Mass ended, the building was empty. There were no social events. There were no young people – no one my own age at all. And everyone there was White. I was the only non-White person there, and I drew stares from everyone.

Still, though, I was lonely, and after a few months I decided to approach the pastor about joining the parish. No one had yet welcomed me or, for that matter, said much of anything to me, but neither had anyone been rude . . . that is, until I spoke with the pastor face-to-face.

"Excuse me, Father, but I'm new to this area and...", I tried to get the attention of Father Bill as he shook the hands of the parishioners after Mass. I was apparently messing up his flow. He shook another hand.

"Pardon me, Father, but I need to talk with you."

Father Bill, clearly irritated, sighed and turned toward me. He neglected, however, to face me. He looked directly over my shoulder, not into my face or eyes. Clearly uncomfortable.

"Yes, what do you need?" he asked as he reached for the next person's hand.

"I attend graduate school at Central University, and I just moved to the area a few . . . two . . . months ago. I . . . . I thought I might . . . join your parish." I stumbled through my words. Expecting to be warmly welcomed into the parish, I was surprised, confused, and starting to have second thoughts.

Father continued to grin – he was grinning at the person behind me – and, between handshakes, managed to respond to me. "Come to the rectory on Wednesday at 10:00 and someone there will help you."

Father still hadn't looked me in the eye. He hadn't told me how glad he was that I wanted to be a part of the parish. I started to object. I had a class on Wednesdays at 9:30 and a lab right afterward. I wouldn't be available on Wednesday until early evening. Perhaps I could come by the rectory on Saturday? . . . But Father Bill was still shaking hands. He'd turned his back on me.

Was he trying to discourage me?

Maybe it was my age. I could well have been the only 22-year-old in the community. Almost everyone else I'd seen was considerably older, ranging in age from early 30s with small children to elderly.

Or maybe it was the fact that I was a student. I'd be leaving the community soon. How much trouble would it have been to sign me up only to lose track of me in a few years?

Or maybe, just maybe . . . was it my race? I'd be the only Black person in the whole parish. I'd never noticed direct evidence of racism in the Church, although I'd heard stories. But this was the first time I'd struck out entirely on my own and tried to gain acceptance on my own merits, not through my family or my college.

Soon after my encounter with Father Bill, I stopped attending Mass. The stares began to make me uncomfortable, and, rather than the peace and calm I used to get from Mass, I just grew agitated.

* * *

Autumn 1985

Two years later I was ready to begin my PhD program. I moved to another small town, and settled into another tiny apartment. Like before, there was a Catholic church close by. Remembering Father Bill, I was reluctant at first, but I still missed my home parish. I started attending Mass again.

The parishioners here were different from the last town. They seemed happy to be at church. They laughed and ate snacks after Mass, talked with each other and smiled. One Sunday, the priest announced a social event – a picnic. Thinking I'd make a few friends, I decided to attend.

When the day arrived, however, I found myself alone. I sat at a table with some young people who appeared to be in their mid twenties, but they ignored me.

I realized then that I was the only Black person in the group. I was making everyone uncomfortable, and noticed them sneaking glances at me, then looking away.

I went to the table with the priest and took matters into my own hands.

"What a wonderful picnic, Father. Do you have these social events often?"

"Oh, yes, every month or so there's something. You're new to this area, aren't you?" he responded.

A good start. Father hadn't tried to avoid me, and I apparently wasn't annoying him.

"Yes, I just moved here a few months ago. I'm enrolled in a PhD program at the University. I've been looking for a parish to join."

Father began to look uncomfortable. He started fidgeting with a napkin, playing with his food. He cleared his throat.

"What should I do to join this parish, Father?" I continued.

"Well, you know, maybe this isn't exactly the right parish for you. There aren't many young people your age in this parish. You'd probably be much happier if you attended Mass at the University. I know someone there. I'll give you Father Sam's number."

Father walked away. He returned a minute later carrying a slip of paper with Father Sam's contact information, and then rushed off to another table.

I never attended another Mass there. I threw away the paper Father had given me. Graduate school is stressful enough. Why add rejection and humiliation to my problems? I put the Catholic Church behind me. It didn't want me. For the next ten years I didn't set foot inside a Catholic church. Frustrated, angry that I'd been rejected, knowing in my heart that it must have been my race that the priests found objectionable, I reacted the way

I thought my mother should have decades earlier. I got on with my life.

LEAVING?

It took me a long time to leave the Church. When I finally did, I felt bitter and forsaken. Good riddance, I thought. The Church never did anything for me! Why should I spend my time, energy, and resources supporting an institution that clearly doesn't want anything to do with me?

But that wasn't entirely true. The Church did a lot for me. No matter how misguided the nuns and priests may have seemed at times, I could never forget the good they did for us when we needed help the most. It was through generous scholarships that we five children were able to attend Catholic schools. Mom could never have afforded the tuition. And the sisters found ways for us to help out around the school for a little extra money to pay for books or supplies. The Church wasn't perfect, but there were some truly good people in it who supported us.

As dysfunctional as it sometimes was, as insane as some of the nuns' stories were, as unjust as it could seem, the Church did at least as much good for me as not. And, even during those years I spent away from it, even when I was at my most resentful, I could never forget how the sisters came to our rescue decades earlier. I could never turn my back completely on the Church that saved our lives when I was a small child.

* * *

October 1992

Grampa passed away. He died in his sleep one night. After years of struggling against Parkinson's disease, losing control over his biological functions, even his speech, he slipped away. The only father figure I had ever known. Gone.

It was hard losing Grampa. Just a month earlier I'd made plans to drive to Detroit for a visit. My mother had been caring for him the last five years. But one thing led to another. I'd recently accepted a job as visiting instructor - my first official college teaching position – and felt like I needed to spend every free moment preparing lessons or grading. I cancelled my plans to go home thinking I'd drive up to see them at Thanksgiving. But Grampa didn't make it to Thanksgiving.

I took it pretty hard. I hadn't seen Grampa in nearly a year, and now I would never see him again. I'd had my chance, and lost it. It was my own fault.

As badly as I felt when Grampa died, my mother took it even harder. He WAS her father, after all. She'd spent the past few years of her life trying to help him stay alive. If I felt like a failure, Mom felt even more like one. And Mom was struggling with schizophrenia. This was one bit of stress too much for her. She snapped.

It didn't happen all at once. At first, she was quiet, withdrawn. Later, she grew antsy. She was short with us on the telephone, didn't want us to bother her when we visited. She told us not to visit, that she wouldn't let us in the door. Then she started acting as if she didn't trust any of us.

About six weeks after Grampa passed, Mom began to believe that all five of her children were conspiring against her. She thought we were planning to take her money. All $138 of her savings. She refused to see us, and when we telephoned her she accused us of all kinds of foolish things – we wanted to kill her for her insurance money, we were sending her telepathic messages to make her sick, we were possessed by the devil and were trying to steal her soul – and then hung up on us. She felt insecure. Afraid she'd have no place to live when the house was sold to pay Grampa's outstanding debts. She actually thought we'd put her out into the street. No matter what we said or did to try to calm her, nothing worked. Then we remembered that Grampa had liked to hunt in his younger, healthier days, and had guns in the house – a 22 rifle and a couple of shotguns. What might Mom do if she got a hold of them? Would she imagine the mailman was trying to harm her if he rang the doorbell with a package? Would she start shooting at dark-colored cars because she believed devils were driving them? Would she shoot one of us if we knocked at her door?

Would she use the guns on herself???

* * *

Christmas 1967

It was an awful time. Dad had left us more than a year earlier, and Mom kept having terrible fights with Gran. We'd been living with Gran and Grampa since Dad walked out on us, but their little five-room house was too small for the eight of us. Mom and Gran were constantly arguing – Gran telling Mom how worthless Dad was, Mom trying to defend him, everyone feeling the strain of trying to raise five small children and three adults on Gran and Grampa's modest incomes. So Mom walked out – she moved us back into the little yellow house that she and Dad had bought. There was still a substantial mortgage on it, but Mom had been trying, with Gran and Grampa's help, to keep up the payments. Mom had no job, but the mortgage company was generous – fancy that! After all, how could they put out a young woman with five small children? The youngest of us, Roland, was barely three.

The stress was too much. Mom began to imagine that we all were in purgatory – the place souls went after they died for their final cleansing before coming face-to-face with God. We'd died soon after Dad left us, Mom insisted, and our souls had gone to purgatory. We ourselves – we who imagined we were living, breathing, eating, going to school, talking with friends – we were just replicates, robots, shells of human beings without a soul, zombies.

As strange as Mom's wild ideas were, we children believed every word. Everyone, that is, except Roger. He didn't believe it for an instant. As for me – I didn't know what to believe. Roger was certain, though. He tried to convince me that Mom was sick, delusional. Pretty sophisticated for an eight-year-old.

"Jeanie, Mom is sick in the head, like Gran says. We're not replicates, we're just regular people."

"But how can Mommy be sick? She doesn't have a fever! Her nose isn't running!" At age six, I was frightened and uncertain. Mom's story scared me, but the thought that she might be wrong scared me even more. If you can't trust Mom, who can you trust?

"I'll prove it to you! Replicates have wires and stuff, not blood, right?"

"Right . . ."

"So I'm gonna take this pin and stick myself and you'll see the blood coming out. That'll prove that I'm real, see?"

"ROGER, NOOOOO!" I started to cry. What if Roger pulled loose some wires? What if the devils that Mom watched every day driving around our neighborhood in black cars got hold of him? How could he take that risk?

But Roger was correct. He pricked himself with the pin, and a few drops of blood came out. No wires, no circuits, no sparks, and no devils. Part of me felt relieved. Another part felt worse than I'd ever felt before. How could Roger be right and Mom wrong?

At that instant, the doorbell rang. The sisters! Mom, afraid the devils would get to Roger and me as we walked home from school, had been keeping us home for several weeks, and the sisters were worried. Sister Teresa, Sister Mary Paul, and their German shepherd dog Blue had come to our house carrying boxes filled with gifts and food.

The sisters broke that tension-filled moment. Mom reluctantly invited them into the house. After all, how could she refuse God's own sisters? And they set up a little Christmas tree in our living room, put gifts under it, and set the box of food in the kitchen. They let us play with Blue – he knew a few tricks – and convinced Mom to let us come back to school after the Christmas holiday. I'll never forget the doll the sisters left for me. You could hold on to her hand and she walked alongside you if you kept her body at just the right angle. It was the best doll I ever owned. More than that, I'll never forget how the sisters' visit struck a normal chord in an otherwise frightening and dysfunctional time.

Mom improved over the holiday. She sent us back to school after Christmas as she had promised. But her progress was short-lived. By February she started becoming delusional again. She gave away our toys and most of our food – replicates didn't need food, after all – and took us out of school. She started praying all the time

– kneeling down in the corner of the living room. Her knees became bruised and discolored. Gran and Grampa grew frantic with worry. When they came over to the house, Mom screamed at them, ordering them out, sometimes throwing at them the things they'd brought. Our pantry was empty, but Mom refused to take food from them. They wanted to get Mom into the hospital for treatment, and were afraid of what she might do to us.

And the sisters came to the rescue again. One night they visited the house, along with our grandparents, and talked Mom into going to the hospital peacefully. We all piled into Grampa's station wagon and drove to the hospital together, Gran on one side of Mom and Sister Mary Paul on the other.

* * *

I'll never forget how the sisters rescued us. Throughout the remainder of the school year, they gave us little things – jars of homemade preserves and cookies, shoes, clothing, crayons. They may have saved our lives. And when Grampa died 25 years later, we wondered if the Church could help us again.

We called Mom's pastor, Father Joseph. Father Joseph didn't know the five of us at all, but Mom had been going to Mass at his church for more than a decade. We explained Mom's problem, how she believed WE were the devils this time, how Grampa had guns in the house and we wanted to get them out so Mom couldn't do anything foolish. We wanted Father Joseph to convince Mom to go to the hospital for observation. Maybe her psychiatrist could adjust her medication.

Father Joseph didn't talk Mom into going to the hospital like the sisters did all those years before. But he did call one of his parishioners to help. Dr. Helen Simmons, a psychologist, agreed to come to the church to talk things over with Mom and the five of us. She got Mom to hand the guns over to us. She convinced her that we weren't devils, just regular people. She persuaded Mom to take her medication – she'd stopped taking it, certain we were trying to poison her. She convinced US that we might have been overreacting – once the guns were out of the house the greatest danger was past, and maybe Mom didn't need to be hospitalized. And she calmed all of us down. Eventually, everything returned to normal.

The church came to the rescue, again.

PART THREE:

THE PRODIGAL SOUL

FAITH WITHOUT WORKS . . .

Even after I left the church, I still encountered people whose spirituality strengthened and validated my own. Some of these people were Catholic, others weren't. But they all felt a tangible connection with the divine and tried to live their lives in ways consistent with what the Catholic church – and a great many other churches, for that matter – professes. Love thy neighbor. Help those in need. Do no harm. While I teetered on the edge of agnosticism, their beliefs forced me to acknowledge the feelings about God and my place in the world that I had been trying for years to deny. I finally returned to the Church, after a long hiatus, because of people I met during this prodigal time.

* * *

Autumn 1986

In graduate school, I learned to think critically about the world. Any inclination to let someone else do my thinking for me was beaten out of me – virtually speaking, of course – as I read the work of ancient historians, questioned their sources and analyzed their motivations. I was expected to make up my own mind, make my own informed judgments, and pick out inaccuracies and inconsistencies. My professors laughed at me when I parroted what I had heard, even if I'd heard it from them! I was expected to seek out information from reliable sources and question everything. If I didn't, my professors surely would, and at some critical and inconvenient time like during my qualifying exams. My mother's responses to life's mysteries – 'the priests and nuns say so therefore it must be true' – melted away into the distant, almost mythic past.

Many a student lost faith during that process. We learned how often gods' names and images were used throughout history to manipulate political situations, how easy it was to influence the masses just by invoking their deities. We learned that gods are virtually always manifestations of a culture's own image of itself, often combined with supernatural powers. But it's all just an image, an illusion. No tangible proof has ever existed for a deity's existence.

You'd have to be a complete fool to believe in God, or at least to admit it in graduate school. My classmates who survived to complete their PhDs were not fools.   Most simply became atheists or agnostics. Those who couldn't face the constant questioning and criticism left without finishing. Some were asked to leave after failing an exam or two. Others packed up at the end of a term after being humiliated a few times during class. Graduate school can be brutal.

One of my classmates began his doctoral degree as a monk. About halfway through, he took a hiatus of several years. When he returned, he told us to call him Jack. He had left the monastery.

For years, I questioned my faith too. All those unlikely miracles the sisters told us about, the great mysteries that only God understood, the rituals and ceremonies we had to take part in so as to avoid eternal damnation, like going to Mass, receiving sacraments – none of it mattered to me anymore. The ceremonies of my childhood had ceased to have any meaning. I strove to put aside childish belief systems, and without proof that God existed, I accepted that He/She might not. Being Catholic, to me, had come to mean membership in a large, powerful organization with restrictive rules, requiring absolute, unconditional loyalty to its leadership, right or wrong, and nothing more. It sure wasn't my ticket to eternal life. I had grown tired of being a pawn.

Yet I held onto the rosaries and the St. Jude statue my mother had given me. They still had sentimental value. And every now and then I prayed – for enlightenment, for clarity of mind. I prayed that I'd pass my qualifying exams. I prayed for help selecting a topic for my dissertation. I prayed for friends who were having difficulty. I prayed for my family. Basically, I prayed when I was troubled. But I didn't say Hail Marys or Our Fathers anymore. I just tried to reach out to what I hoped might be a real divine presence, a presence who might be listening to me.

* * *

My dissertation chair, Julian, and I became close friends. He was a supportive director, even to the point of standing up for me when one of my committee members started giving me a hard time for no apparent reason. Was it racism? Neither of us knew for certain, but Julian told him that his services were no longer needed when he refused to sign off on my defense date, claiming that I had too many graphs in my dissertation. Julian – not Catholic, but a person with strong spiritual convictions and a clear sense of right and wrong – unwittingly taught me how to find a balance between a scholar's essential skepticism and a human being's spirituality. We talked about the divine on many occasions.

* * *

Sunday morning, Summer 1987

"I observed the Greek Orthodox service this morning, Julian. It was a lot different from what I expected."

"How so?"

"The language was unusual. I couldn't make out a lot of the vocabulary. And there was quite a bit of chanting. It seemed very formalized, highly ritualized. I though it would be more like a Catholic service."

"Good observations. The language they speak during religious services is called *katharevousa*. It's also called 'High Greek', and is used only in special cultural contexts, like religious rituals. It's archaic, much closer to ancient Greek than modern. If you think of the language as Classical Greek with modern pronunciations you'll probably have less difficulty understanding it. Where were you in the church during the service?"

"In the back. I tried to pay attention to what the women were doing so I could mimic them."

"No – their rituals are sacred to them. Don't ever give the impression that you're mimicking. They might think you're mocking. And whether you personally believe or not, never mock. Visitors are usually welcomed as long as they don't interfere with the service. Just stand in the back and observe. They'll know you're not Greek Orthodox, but they won't mind as long as they believe you respect them."

Julian had as much reason to feel alone as I did. An openly gay man in one of the most traditional and conservative academic disciplines, sometimes the homophobia of the academy seemed to close in on him.

Generally as cynical as the rest of my professors, Julian wasn't so quick to dismiss the 'exceptions.'

"There are some things that defy rational explanation," he said to me one day. "The stigmata, for example. People who begin bleeding from their hands, maybe also their feet and sides, with no biological reason. I've never found a satisfactory explanation for it."

"Maybe it's psychological." I responded, attempting to maintain an appropriately suspicious position.

"Maybe. But there are other phenomena that defy explanation. Human psychology can't explain all of them."

"Julian, are you saying that you believe in miracles? You believe in God?"

"Part of me does. I'm not a member of any church. They're all corrupt institutions anyway. Most don't want gays and lesbians in their congregations, and God knows I don't need them. But sometimes, especially when I'm traveling overseas by myself, I visit a church. I sit alone for a while. It calms me, helps me feel at peace. I like to imagine I'm communing with God. Maybe that's psychological too. But it helps. I feel better afterward."

Julian and I were a lot alike. We both knew that we didn't fit any of society's molds. Mainstream churches wanted mainstream members – White, middle or upper class, heterosexual, married, conservative, passive, and of average intelligence. Neither of us belonged. And we both had to deal with living as an 'outsider' in an otherwise homogeneous world – the world of the academy.

Julian had a reputation among the graduate students for being hard and inflexible. He expected his students to be precise and thorough, and didn't hesitate to embarrass his students to the point of tears in the classroom. He also didn't mind interfering on a personal level if he felt someone was in trouble.

One student, Jenny, had a particularly hard time adjusting to the rigor of graduate school. She developed anorexia, and almost wasted away, losing 30 or 40 pounds over the course of a semester. She couldn't have weighed more than 80 pounds when she was at her worst. Julian talked with her a few times. Julian was director of graduate studies for our department, and when her condition continued to degenerate, he refused to sign her course registration card, forcing her into a leave of absence. He wouldn't allow her to return, he said, until she'd received clearance from her physician.

The rest of the faculty was relieved. No one wanted to see Jenny get sicker and sicker. All of them wanted her to continue with her studies, although there was some talk of getting 'out of the kitchen if you can't stand the heat'. But no one dared talk with Jenny about her problem – it was a personal matter, they all insisted. Only Julian did something about it. Not caring what anyone else thought about it, indifferent to the many who believed he was out of line, ignoring Jenny's pleading, tears, and eventual curses, he did what he thought was right, and what no one else had the guts to do. He probably saved her life.

Julian showed me that there are many ways of knowing the divine. We may never find it in religious texts and prayer cards. We have to look inside, deep into our hearts. Once we find it, we can use it to guide our actions. None of the other faculty, even those who were regular churchgoers, cared enough about Jenny to do anything. Only Julian did. I hope I have the strength of character to do what he did when/if the time comes.

ANOTHER SERMON

"*Because the divine has entered the human situation in Jesus and has issued God's judgment against poverty, sickness, and oppression, persons who fight against these inhumanities become instruments of God's word. This is the dialectic of Christian thought: God enters into the social context of human existence and appropriates the ideas and actions of the oppressed as God's own. When this event of liberation occurs in thought and praxis, the words and actions of the oppressed become the Word and Actions of God. They no longer belong to the oppressed. Indeed, the word of the oppressed becomes God's Word insofar as the former recognize it not as their own but as given to them through divine grace. The oppressed have been elected, not because of the intrinsic value of their word or action but because of God's grace and freedom to be with the weak in troubled times. Thus the source of the distinction between the oppressed and the oppressors, the elected and the excluded, is not a body of rational principles derived from human experience, but is rather, God the Creator and Redeemer of human life"* *(Cone 1997:90).*

* * *

Not every sermon I heard growing up was misogynistic, politicized, or racist. Some were stirring and insightful. The best sermons were those denouncing oppression. Whenever a priest interpreted the Word through the eyes of the oppressed, I could feel an intellectual and spiritual connection with the Word. The very first such sermon I heard was during Black History month – a sermon given by a Black priest. I would learn that, by and large, the sermons that held the most meaning for me were those delivered by those who had been victims of oppression. They could interpret God's word in a way that had relevance to me. And, as a Black woman, Black priests who understood, who had lived the trials of Blacks, usually connected with me better than the rest.

Of course, not every Black priest preaches good sermons. I've heard a few dreadful ones. And not every White priest is bad. Some are phenomenal. But those who've lived their lives fighting some of the same battles that I encounter every day, through much the same lenses similar to my own, can find ways to make the Word of God resonate in a meaningful and memorable way.

* * *

February 1995

Black History Month! The college had begun inviting prominent Black priests from all over the country to say Mass for the community during this month. The church is packed every time. You have to get there fifteen minutes early to find a seat. The newly-formed Gospel choir sings traditional spirituals, and the Black students and faculty take part in every ministry – lectors, greeters, ushers, acolytes, and bearers of the gifts.

This month, Father Theodore from New Orleans is our guest celebrant. The readings are from Job, Paul, and Mark.

* * *

"Job is one of my favorite books of the Old Testament. Poor, poor Job! You remember what happens to him, don't you, brothers and sisters? Job did everything right. He was holy and upright, and God rewarded him with all the things that he wanted. Then, out of the blue, God takes everything away! Just like that!" He snaps his fingers.

"He lost his property, his family, everything. And you know what's the worst part? It had nothing to do with him. Not a thing! You know why it happened, don't you?"

The congregation looks at Father Theodore expectantly.

"Because God was messing around! Playing games with the devil! It didn't matter that Job loved God and followed his commandments. He did everything he was supposed to do - studied hard, got to work on time, did his homework, met his deadlines, paid his bills on time, drove the speed limit – followed *all* the rules!

Father Theodore speaks slowly and deliberately. "IT HAD NOTHING TO DO WITH HIM!"

He pauses.

"You all know where I'm coming from, don't you? You know *exactly* how it feels to do *everything* right and still fail! Because we've all been there, haven't we?"

The students nod their heads. The faculty members look at each other and shake theirs sadly.

"Job says, 'I'm so tired during the day I can hardly stand, and when I go to bed I'm so restless I can't sleep!' He says, 'My days drag on without hope, and I shall not see happiness again.'

"Now, THOSE are some sad words, aren't they, brothers and sisters?"

Father's question is answered with a scattering of 'Amens' and 'Uh Huhns'.

"Who all knows what happens to Job? Do you, Sister?" Father asks a student in the front row. She shakes her head. "What about you, Brother?" The next student shrugs his shoulders. "Doesn't anybody know what happens to Job?"

Someone toward the back of the church shouts, "He endures, doesn't lose faith, and gets everything back!"

Father smiles. "Alright! I KNEW one of you all would know!" Everyone laughs.

"That's right! Job says to God, 'I don't know why I had to endure all that, but it's ok. God took everything away from me, but I still won't renounce Him. I'll still try to be righteous, I'll still be an enemy to the wicked man, I'm still gonna try to do the right thing!'"

Father pauses again, then continues. "Don't you know how Job felt? You do everything right, but everything goes wrong. How would YOU feel?

"I know how I'd feel! I'd be TEMPTED to say, 'Doggone it, what does it matter? I do the right thing and I get nothing but bad luck and misery! Why should I bother? I don't even care no more. I'm just gonna do any old thing! Maybe I'll start lying, or cheating, or stealing, 'cause the results will be the same! It doesn't matter!' Is that what I should say, brothers and sisters?"

He has everyone's attention. They're leaning forward a little, all eyes on him. "No!" they say all in one voice. Father chuckles a little and responds.

"No! You STILL have to do the right thing! Even when nothing goes your way! We don't always know why things don't work out no matter how hard we try. Sometimes it's the devil, just like it was with Job!

Sometimes Satan puts a little seed of hatred in *The Man's* heart to mess around with ya. But don't let that devil put that seed in YOUR heart! Don't give up hope, brothers and sisters! Don't ever stop trying. Today's Psalm reads, 'He heals the heartbroken and binds up their wounds. He tells the number of stars, and calls each one by name.'

"Mark's Gospel reading tells us how Jesus healed lepers, He cast out demons. How do you think that leper felt in the Gospel? You think he might have felt a little like Job?"

A few scattered 'Uh huhns' and vigorous nods are Father's response.

"You know he did! Was probably thinking about Job as soon as he realized what was happening. Woke up one morning, notices he's getting a rash. The next day his family and friends are stoning him, making him leave town and wear a bell around his neck so everyone can hear when he's coming. One day he has a house, and a family who loves him, and a community of friends to laugh with, go out to dinner with, who trust him. The next day he has to beg for crumbs. But Jesus healed him. That leper didn't lose *his* faith. God is with us, whether we realize it or not. God heals us. No matter how low we feel, how much we're hurting, how many battles we've fought, how lost we are. God will still heal us. When you're at your lowest, don't give up hope. Don't ever give up on God. 'Cause God will <u>never</u> give up on you. Amen"

Father Theodore's message stayed with me a long time. I would need it sooner than I realized.

NEW FACULTY

August 1995

The start of a new school year. The fledgling Africana Studies Program hosted an opening reception for Black faculty, students, and administrators. Punch, pastries, fresh fruit, and conversation for a few hours as we got reconnected after several months absence. And the 'welcome back' reception was a great opportunity to introduce the new Black faculty.

This year, Father Richard, who'd recently completed his PhD in Church History, joins the faculty. Father Richard's recruitment talk was on the history of Black priests in the United States. It's a long, sad story of perseverance in the face of abuse and neglect, hope in the face of hatred, sometimes early death under the stress of trying to minister to an unwelcoming and unresponsive parish. I served on the committee that had recruited him to campus, so I struck up a conversation.

"Richard, I'm curious about your research. How did you get your bishop to approve it? Wasn't it too controversial? And what about the impact on you personally? Didn't it bring you down?"

Richard smiles and shakes his head. "It *was* depressing. And I had to fight a battle or two. But it's a story that had to be told, and my bishop eventually came around."

"I have to know something . . . if it's too personal I'll understand. How can you stay committed to the Church knowing the history the way you do?"

Richard stares off into the distance, no doubt remembering some of the more unpleasant events he wrote about, maybe thinking about his own personal stories. After a long moment, he responds.

"I guess there's no easy answer, but maybe this is the beginning of one. I'm a convert, you know. I joined the church when I was 15 years old. My parents were Methodists, and they were stunned when I told them I wanted to become a Catholic. I'd been attending Catholic school, and I'd gone to Catholic Church a few times. And everything about Catholicism struck a chord with me. I wanted to be part of something that, for me, was so wonderful. I was old enough to make my own decisions about faith, and my mother grudgingly accepted it. Then, just a few years later, I told her I wanted to be a priest and stunned her again! The Catholic Church was such a good fit for me. The doctrines, the rituals, the brotherhood – it all made sense.

"By the time I was in seminary, I grew more aware of racism. I'd been shielded from it by my folks before then. So I joined some activist organizations, clipped newspaper articles about racism and posted them on bulletin boards. I pretty much made an ass of myself! I don't know if I did any good, but I got a lot off my chest. And I found quite a few advocates, White *and* Black.

"That's why I chose this topic for my research. The canons, the teachings – I still believe that, if you want to do good in this world, if you want to live a good life and influence others in a positive way, if you want to live your life in a way that helps you and others grow closer to the divine, the Catholic Church, for me, is the only way to do that.

"I know the Church isn't perfect. It won't be perfect long after I die – it'll never be perfect. People are people, after all. They're flawed, and some of them have given up trying to do the right thing. That's as true for priests and nuns as it is for the laity. It's sometimes easier to go along with peer pressure than it is to stand up and speak out against something, even if you know it's wrong. The way I see it though, I could either give in and let them keep me from something truly good, or I could keep fighting the 'good fight', and maybe be a good influence on people who are on the verge of losing their way. That's the path I've chosen. But the only way to do that effectively is to acknowledge the past. So my research is pretty damn depressing! But it's true, and it has to see the light of day. Once the bad stuff is out in the open, we can figure out where we went wrong, and how to effect positive change."

Richard and I became friends. Over the years, I would find myself thinking back to his research, and wondering about the fortitude it took to submit to an institution that had oppressed and maligned his own people – *our* people – for so many generations. They say faith can move mountains. Work like Richard's is helping to move the Church in the right direction regarding equality.

MINISTRY FOR BLACK STUDENTS

Do Blacks require different forms of ministry than Whites do? I've worked at five different colleges with student ministry programs. At each one, that same question gets raised. How seriously the answer is considered, however, is another matter.

In a perfect world, ministry programs wouldn't need to be tailor-made for different kinds of students. Men, women, Blacks, Whites, Asians, Hispanics, Native Americans, old, young, rich, poor – they would all hear the same message of love, tolerance, forgiveness, service, and compassion, and they would all understand how to apply that message in their daily lives. Unfortunately, we don't live in that world.

In our world, we're still living with the by-products of racialized slavery and gender inequality. Even today, three decades after the woman's movement, women are still expected to apologize for supporting 'Women's Liberation'. The word 'feminist' is used to insult women who become uncomfortably vocal. The median *per capita* incomes for Blacks are nearly 42% lower than they are for Whites. Women on average earn only 76% what men earn (U.S. Census Bureau). Blacks are nearly seven times more likely to spend time in jail than Whites (Bureau of Justice Statistics 2006).

And then there's the pulpit. Things are better now than they were twenty years ago. You'd have to search long and hard to find a priest today that still publicly supports racist attitudes and spouts them from the pulpit. But they're still out there. My own generation, and that of my mother, is marked by the early days of hearing about the curse of Ham, about slavery being a just punishment for some ancestor's sin. Some people still believe that. I've had students, as recently as the year 2005, who were told they weren't welcome in White parishes. They heard this from some of the parishioners *and* the priests. I've known of Black Catholics who were refused Holy Communion when visiting a White church while traveling. But I've never heard of White visitors being questioned or refused the Eucharist, or being told they're unwelcome.

So, I'd have to say yes to the question about ministry. We do need to consider the special needs of Black students when we design ministry programs. We can't assume that the programs that shape the minds of the White majority will work for Blacks, that Blacks will hear the same message that Whites hear, that Blacks have the same needs that Whites have. Until we live in that perfect world, we have to keep dealing with the social inequality that our world produces.

* * *

Autumn 1995

6:30 in the evening. Time to go home after a long workday. Before heading over to the parking lot, however, I decide to stop by the office of my friend Julia, the assistant director of collegiate ministry. Julia had recently been charged with developing an ethnic ministry program for the various groups of students. She'd asked for my support, and I wanted to plan a lunchtime 'brainstorming session' for later in the week. A 40-something brown-skinned Black woman who struck nearly everyone she met as both maternal and professional, Julia was an easy person to trust.

"Jean, do you think you can help me with a room reservation? I need a room big enough for about 100 people with movable desks – I want the students to work in small groups."

"Sure, I know of two or three classrooms that fit that description. What're you planning?"

"The Black students want to start a Bible study group. Last week I put out a sign-up sheet, and already I've got 78 people!"

Wow! "How many Black Catholic students do we have? I figured there were only about 20 or 30. Aren't they getting what they need in Simmons' *Introduction to the Bible* class?"

Julia looks at me sidelong and grimaces as we both start laughing loudly. Father Wilson Simmons, a White 'old-school' priest nearing or maybe past retirement age, approaches study of the Bible pretty much the same way our high school catechism teachers did. The White students tolerate him, the Black students hate him. Every now and again the 'Curse of Ham' creeps into his lectures. We'll both be glad when he retires for good.

"You're right, we've only got 27 Black Catholic students. But there are close to 100 Black students interested in the ministry programs. Most of them aren't Catholic. They just want a safe place to talk about their faith. The interfaith dialogs that they've set up have gone extremely well – I'm so proud of them! And these are the kids we need to spend time on. They've really been neglected over the years."

In the past, Collegiate Ministry had been resistant to the idea of interfaith dialogs, fearful that they would be perceived as advocating non-Catholic faith traditions.

"Your bosses have changed." I say. "They're more progressive than they used to be."

"Oh no, girl, they don't know anything about it! No, I have to ease them into it. Right now, Father James thinks we're working on converting the non-Catholics! He doesn't realize that they're finding common ground. And, truth is, some of them *have* talked about converting. But that's not what the interfaith dialogs are about. I just want the children to be comfortable, to have a place to grow in their own faith, where they won't be labeled 'the non-Catholics', which you know just about translates into 'heathen' around here. Eventually, I want to arrange for buses to take the students to traditionally Black Catholic churches, AND to Baptist and AME churches too, but that'll take some time. I asked Father James about it last month, and he about had a fit! So we've got to move slowly."

Eventually Julia would accomplish all her goals, *except* the buses to the Protestant churches. She would succeed, however, in arranging car pools. By the end of the school year, Julia's monthly Black Catholic Masses would be the best-attended Catholic services on campus. And people from all ethnicities took part in the service, not just Black students.

Later in the year, we celebrate Julia's success at our favorite Chinese food restaurant. As we start making plans for the following year, I ask her about her faith.

"Doesn't it bother you that you spend so much time supporting a Church that has a history of misogyny and racism? You really believe in what you're doing. How can you?"

"The message of the Church is all about love and tolerance. If you read the Bible, especially the New Testament, it comes through loud and clear.

"We all know that the Church isn't perfect. The people who run it aren't perfect, so how can it be? *WE* know it, so, on a grassroots level, we can do something about it. When students complain about some priest's misogyny, we tell 'em the truth. The Church does have some misogynistic policies, and it needs US to challenge the status quo. Nothing will ever change if we leave the Church or ignore it. And if a professor is teaching misogyny or racism, we challenge him. We support the students who complain. We're the key to the solution, Jean. We just have to remember where we came from, and keep our eyes on the prize."

YOU JUST DON'T FIT

"[D]espite earning doctorates in ever-increasing numbers, many women and persons of color are eschewing academic careers altogether or exiting the academy prior to the tenure decision because both groups experience social isolation, a chilly environment, bias, and hostility. Their common concerns include their limited opportunities to participate in departmental and institutional decision-making; excessive and 'token' committee assignments; infrequent occasions to assume leadership positions or achieve an institutional presence; research that's trivialized and discounted; lack of mentors; and little guidance about the academic workplace or the tenure process" (Trower and Chait 2002).

You'd think a Catholic institution would be above all that. That's what I thought. I was in for a rude awakening.

* * *

Autumn 1997

After I defended my doctoral dissertation, I tried to move out of the administrative position I'd held for four years and into a tenure-track position on the faculty. The department I'd be joining, however, was reluctant to make me an offer.

They made a number of excuses. They said they didn't need another teacher for the lower level courses, even though they'd been hiring an adjunct to teach those same courses for several years. They didn't have room for more courses in my specialty area in the curriculum, even though I'd been teaching 300- and 400-level courses in my specialty for a few years for them, my classes consistently filled, and no one else in the department could teach my areas. They were unsure of my credentials, even though I'd earned my PhD at one of the top institutions in my discipline, as good a school or better than most of the other faculty in the department had attended. Bottom line was, I 'just didn't fit,' in the words of my dean as he broke the news to me.

My mentor, David, a senior Black faculty member in my division but not in that department, wanted to know the decision. I told him.

"You're kidding me. What exactly did you ask for?"

"What every new faculty member gets, David", I replied. "The rank of assistant professor, a 2-3 teaching load, the same salary I'm getting now – nothing more – and a six-year tenure clock. That's it."

"I just can't see why they wouldn't say yes!"

David had urged me to approach the dean to request this change. We both knew what a dead-end position I had – great for someone with a Master's degree or lower, but for a Black woman with a PhD in a scholarly discipline? I could do better. And I would never advance. I'd already hit the glass ceiling. The only future for me lay in the

scholarly ranks. And our president had recently
announced an initiative to recruit more faculty of color
and women. The time seemed right to make a move.

"I've seen your course evaluations, and they're good!
As good as anyone else's in the whole division. Better than
some! And I read your article that was just accepted. It's
good too. The journal you sent it to is refereed. What
excuse can they possibly have?" David doesn't want to
admit what we both suspect – know – is the truth.

"They refuse to acknowledge the article, David," I
told him. "Twice the dean told me, 'You should try to
publish some of your research'. Both times I reminded
him that I've already been doing that. None of the other
junior faculty members in the department has published,
but they're blind to mine. What should I do?"

David was quiet. We both knew what my next step
had to be, but neither of us wanted to say it. Instead we
stared out his window for a long moment.

David had been at the institution for ten years, and
he'd seen a lot. More than he wanted to. The only Black
full professor in the whole college, he'd been hired with his
rank and tenure. In the ten years he'd been there, not one
Black assistant professor had ever earned tenure there.
"It'd be easier to win the Nobel prize than it is to get
tenure here if you're Black" – that was the bitter joke that
went around the school.

David may have been a high-ranking full professor,
but his colleagues treated him as though he were just
another assistant professor. He was shouted down in
committee meetings by associate professors, his junior
colleagues. More often, he was simply ignored. Few if any
projects or initiatives he proposed were supported. He was
very much on his own at our institution. He'd felt the sting
of racism all his life. He never grew accustomed to it.

Normally a quiet, private man, David had earned a reputation as the most vocal faculty member on matters of diversity. He pushed harder than anyone else to diversify the curriculum, the faculty, and the student-body. He wrote letters, met with the president and deans, even created new courses with multicultural themes. He spent time with graduate students and junior faculty from all over the region, giving advice, reviewing their work prior to publication. A devout Catholic, he criticized the Church and our institution for what he saw as racist practices, practices that had a trickle-down effect on the curriculum and the students. David believed in the message of the Church, but not in the habits of the administration. He lived his beliefs.

"You earned your bachelor's degree from this institution, didn't you?" David asks.

"Yes."

"So, you're Catholic, Black, a woman, an alumna, a graduate of a high-ranking doctoral institution – higher ranking than this institution is – and you're published. All the qualities they say they're looking for."

He pauses, then continues in a voice so quiet I have to strain to hear him.

"What's it gonna take? You couldn't be a better fit. How can they not see this for what it really is?" The look on his face was pained. We shared a glance. He looked away almost immediately, but not before I caught a glimpse of a tear in his eye. My own eyes began to water. After another long moment, he continues.

"You know what you have to do. You've got to leave. There's no place for you here. After this, even if you appealed to the president and managed to find a way to twist their arms into placing you on a tenure track, it wouldn't matter. They don't see you as a fellow scholar, or a colleague. They're seeing you as a Black woman, a threat to their little fiefdom. They'd be looking for a way to deny you tenure. You have to find another position somewhere else before they find a way to do you harm."

". . . I know."

"And THIS is the way they build what they call 'Catholic character.' I can't believe it."

David worked hard to correct what he saw as injustices in the academy. Between teaching, research, and mentoring, he often put in 15-hour days trying to complete his regular tasks in addition to helping junior faculty members unravel the double-talk that we often heard from our senior colleagues, going to bat for those of us who were too vulnerable to speak up for ourselves. Ultimately, he worked himself into an early grave trying to make a difference. He personified Catholic character in a way that no one else at the institution did.

We sat together for a few more minutes. Eventually I thanked David and asked him if he'd help me prepare my materials to go on the market the following year. He said he would. And I thought about Catholic character as I walked, very slowly, back to my office.

PART FOUR:

GOODBYE AGAIN?

THE LETTER

Winter 2005

Solomon, our deacon of 23 years, had died. Poor Sol. He was 78 years old and in pretty good health – that is, until his wife Sara passed away earlier in the year. They teased each other a lot, but everyone could see how devoted they were to each other. Their eyes lit up whenever the other came into a room. And you hardly ever saw them alone. They were always together. So when Sara left him, Sol was alone and heartbroken. On August 12th, just six months later, he died in his sleep. They were together at last, for eternity this time.

St. Sebastian's needed a deacon. We had relied on old Sol for a long time. He always came when one of us called. He spent time visiting the sick, he talked with us when we were troubled. He opened his home to us when there was a crisis, offering his spare room when out-of-town relatives arrived for a funeral, or when a troubled teen stormed away after an argument with parents. We trusted Sol and Sara. We loved them.

John had long considered the diaconate. Sol, who had recently been complaining that there was too much work for a single deacon, had encouraged him, and our former pastor, Father Ed, agreed to support him. So John applied to the diocesan lay ministry program. There were mix-ups with the paperwork, however. Deadlines were missed, and John had to wait another year before he could begin. But during that year, Father Ed, our pastor, was transferred to another parish nearly an hour away. Father George was called in to replace him.

Father George was great at first. Young, handsome, with thick reddish-blond hair, perfect white teeth, and the soft accent of a Southern gentleman, he stood in stark contrast to 60-something Father Ed. Father George was enthusiastic and had a pretty good sense of humor. Somewhere in his mid-thirties, he'd been a priest for about seven years, and St. Sebastian's was his first appointment as pastor. His good looks and energy made a fine first impression, but his inexperience in matters of parish politics made him easy prey for the lay advisory council, which saw him as someone they could 'mold.' They ensnared him almost immediately.

As the months passed, Fr. George had less and less time for us. He was responsible for another parish too, a larger one, and St. Sebastian's was self-sufficient enough that Father George wasn't needed for the day-to-day problems. The Committee of Parochial Advisors (CPA), St. Sebastian's lay advisory council, handled everything as we had when Father Ed was in charge. We only saw Father George a couple of times each month for Sunday Mass. And, although Father George was friendly enough and never cross with any of us, he didn't spend much time with us either. He never stayed after Mass for coffee and cake at the social hour, never went to our bi-monthly potluck suppers, never participated in our fundraisers, never took time to talk with the children during CCD classes. We liked him at first, but we didn't really love him. He was too distant. The only people he interacted with regularly were a few members of the CPA, and they were a powerful minority. They made all the decisions about the collection money and how it was to be used, often without consulting the rest of the parish. The most powerful members of the CPA also took an active dislike to certain other parishioners, apparently on socioeconomic grounds. They didn't like the ones who weren't at least middle-class. Elitism, it seemed, was alive and well in our parish.

John and his family were in the wrong socioeconomic class. At the other end of the ladder, John and his wife Beverly both worked long hours, struggling to make ends meet. Still, John took his calling seriously. He talked with Father George about it, explaining that Father Ed had agreed to support him. He showed him the paperwork that had been filled out but that had missed the previous year's deadline. They talked briefly about his calling.

Father George agreed to support John, but only provisionally. One of the conditions was financial. George wouldn't allow the money to come from the regular collection. John's support would have to come from a special collection.

We had to raise at least $1700 to pay for John's tuition, books, and supplies for a year. Over the course of the next month, therefore, announcements were made and the parish was invited to give money earmarked for John in specially designated envelopes. By the end of the month, $2900 had been collected, enough for nearly two years. Surely a powerful statement of parochial support!

Everything was arranged. John entered the program and started attending the twice-weekly evening classes. He was doing well too – he received excellent comments on all his work. But by the time January rolled around and John needed an evaluation letter from his pastor, Father George had changed his mind. He wrote John a letter saying that he'd decided not to support him any more. John could finish out the year, but then he would have to withdraw from the program. He never gave John a chance to talk with him about it privately, but offered to discuss it with him in a closed meeting before the CPA. John declined.

Most of the parish was incensed. How dare Father George challenge our support! How dare he oppose John's calling, flout Sol's and Father Ed's good judgment! Some parishioners had known John for 20 years. We'd given our money specifically for his education. We'd made our support known publicly. Father George didn't know any of us, hadn't taken the time even to get to know John. All that he'd done of substance in the year he'd been with us was interfere when we were trying to support our friend and fill the gap created by Sol's death.

John's supporters wrote letters to Father George. Some sent copies to the bishop. But it didn't make any difference. Father George was unyielding. He wouldn't reconsider, and he wouldn't explain why. "I have my reasons and I'm under no obligation to share them with you. They're confidential." That's what he said at the special CPA meeting that the whole parish was invited to attend when we insisted on an explanation. Had the bishop cracked down on the rising number of aspiring deacons? Was St. Sebastian's too small to warrant its own deacon? Maybe our bishop had been waiting for Sol to pass on, and never intended to replace him. Or maybe there was something troubling about John's application? About his progress? About his credentials?

We suspected, however, that the CPA had managed somehow to demonize John. They had Father George's ear in a way that the rest of us did not. But we would never find out for certain.

John was disappointed, but he knew we'd done all we could. He started attending Mass at Father Ed's parish – he still continued in regular attendance at St. Sebastian's – and when Father Ed caught wind of what had happened, he offered to continue the support that St. Sebastian's had begun. So John never had to miss a term.

But when Father George found out, he was furious. Unaccustomed to having authority at all, he recoiled at the threat of having his first taste of it challenged. He sent John another letter saying that he could no longer do service work of any sort at St. Sebastian's. Father George didn't say it in so many words, but he pretty much showed John the door. He made it clear that John wasn't welcome to participate in our parish. I almost didn't believe it until John showed me the letter. I found myself thinking back to the times I was shunned all those years ago.

So I wrote a letter of my own to Father George. I let him know how wrong I thought he was to treat a long-time member of St. Sebastian's that way and how I believed his reaction was unreasonable. I mailed the letter on that cold January day at the post office on highway 46.

John was one of the first people at St. Sebastian's to make me feel welcome. He encouraged me to put together a presentation on Blacks in the Church during the first February I was a member, despite the fact that nearly all the parishioners are White. So, in my mind at least, an attack on John was almost as bad as an attack on me. I wasn't sure I wanted to remain a member of a parish whose pastor was treating my friend so badly when he had done nothing to deserve it.

WHY?

Racism. The same racism we were taught to avoid as children. The same racism that so many of my students refuse to acknowledge today. It still exists. I have many childhood memories of the Church. Many are good memories – singing in the choir, going on parish field trips, being asked to serve as lector. Some are bad – the silencing of doubts, the fear of questioning. My memories of racism in the Church, however, are among my most poignant and troubling.

How did racism become so entrenched in Catholic teachings? From the pulpit to the classroom, we receive conflicted messages: We are all equal in the eyes of God; God loves us all the same no matter who we are or where we come from; we all have the same free will, the same aptitude for good and for evil.

But almost in the same breath, we're told that Blacks are *unequal*. That we're cursed. That we must work twice as hard as everyone else to work off that curse. That our ancestors, slaves dragged from their homes and families, brought to the U.S. against their will, were supposed to have obeyed their masters 'with fear and trembling, in sincerity of heart, as to Christ' (Ephesians 6.5). If they resisted their enslavement, they were fighting against God. And even today, when we buy into the rhetoric of our own oppression, we're told to stay out of the church. We're not welcome. We make 'good' people uncomfortable. No matter how hard we try, how much we aim to please, how good we are, we're never good enough. Proper mainstream society doesn't want us in its presence.

Those were the messages of my formative years. From my mother's teachers, to Father Grayson's sermon, to Dr. Simon's Bible class, to the images of Jesus that we were expected to revere, to the attitudes of our teachers during White flight, to the attempts of White faculty to exclude Black faculty from their ranks, the message has been the same. Even now, decades after the Civil Rights movement, I hear the same message. Jo Anne Tardy describes hearing the same message growing up as a Catholic in New Orleans of the 1940s and 50s (Tardy 2006). Even our own congressmen have endorsed racist attitudes (Louis 2002; Raspberry 2005; Daifallah 2003).

Albert Raboteau (2004) explains the phenomenon from an historical perspective. Early in the history of our country, there was a tendency among a few Protestant groups to interpret the message of the Gospel as a leveling force, to help balance the social order, and to treat Blacks and Whites equally in the eyes of God. These early Protestants condemned slavery as inconsistent with the message of Jesus. Their voices, however, were drowned out in the face of the economic reality that the New World had become dependent upon slave labor. For most Whites, slavery was considered necessary and just. Indeed, it was valued as a powerful good endorsed by the Gospel, "sanctioned by Scripture and capable of producing a Christian social order based on the observance of mutual duty, slave to master and master to slave. It was the ideal of the antebellum plantation mission to create such a rule of gospel order by convincing slaves and masters that their salvation depended upon it" (Raboteau 2004:152). The perceived economic exigency mandated a religious sanction for an unjust institution. Political and economic ideologies helped craft a religious ideology.

Prior to 1865, therefore, the institution of slavery was represented – marketed – as a just punishment for evil. Those who practiced it imagined slavery to be consistent with God's plan. Now, however, slavery is illegal, and was condemned by Pope Leo XIII in 1890. Slavery is no longer directly responsible for the treatment of Blacks in America. Instead, it's the attitude that our blackness somehow translates into inferiority, an attitude shaped by the ideology of slavery, to be sure, but one that has developed a life of its own more than a century after slavery ended in the United States.

In the Classical world, black skin was considered beautiful. Frank Snowden's (1991) research with the representation of Blacks in antiquity has demonstrated that, in the ancient Greco-Roman world, skin color was not considered a pejorative. Black skin was, at the least, viewed as an interesting characteristic, and at best, an exotically beautiful feature. Skin color did not translate into slave status. It was not a sign of evil. It was not a taint. It simply was.

Cain Hope Felder (1991:132) notes that, by the fifth century CE, the Bible was being used to support or justify political ideologies, a process he refers to as *sacralization*. It is in fifth and seventh century Midrash documents, e.g., that we find reference to the stain of blackness. And by the seventeenth century – at about the same time that

Black slaves were being brought to the New World – "the idea persisted that the blackness of Africans was due to a curse, and that idea reinforced and sanctioned the enslavement of Blacks."

Shawn Copeland takes Felder's observations to another level. Not only was blackness viewed as a kind of taint, but the obverse became true for European philosophers, and their ideas took hold. Kant, Voltaire, and Jefferson, among others, supported the notion that light skin color was a sign that white men were intellectually, morally, culturally, and spiritually superior. This gave them the right to enslave people with black skin, who were meant by nature for eternal servitude: "Within Christianity, blackness came to insinuate dirt and filth, evil and sin, guilt and moral degradation, death and the diabolical.... Many African peoples, both on the continent and in the diaspora, internalized these negative and, fundamentally, self-destructive meanings. Too many of us thought that our black skin rendered us base, dirty, polluted, ugly, inferior" (Copeland 1998:121).

That may be the worst crime of all – that generations of Black children grew to adulthood believing in their inferiority. Octavia Butler (2005:133) perhaps says it best: "There seems to be an unwritten rule, hurtful and at odds with the realities of American culture. It says you aren't supposed to wonder whether as a Black person, a Black woman, you really might be inferior – not quite bright enough, not quite quick enough, not quite good enough to do the things you want to do. Though, of course, you do wonder. You're supposed to *know* you're as good as anyone. And if you don't know, you aren't supposed to admit it."

The curse of Ham has been used for centuries to rationalize the oppression of Black peoples. The message has been preached from the pulpit countless times. And

Blacks have accepted it. The curse of Ham is a profound statement of God's unwillingness to forgive us the sins of our ancestors. It justifies centuries of Black subjugation at the hands of Whites, who, after all, are only helping to ensure that God's will is done. Our oppressors are the very hands of God.

Felder shows that the curse of Ham is a prime example of sacralization. A biblical story used throughout the centuries to support the enslavement of a people, when in reality, religion had nothing to do with it. Economics brought about slavery; religion was twisted after the fact to justify it. Black people were never cursed in the Ham story. In fact, Ham himself was never cursed. Noah, in response to Ham's disobedience, cursed Ham's son Canaan.

The so-called curse of Ham never existed.

"Cursed be Canaan, the lowest of slaves shall he be to his brothers. He [Noah] also said: Blessed be the Lord, the God of Shem. Let Canaan be his slave" (Gen 9.25-26).

The cursed son, Canaan, fathers a vast group of peoples, including Sodom and Gomorrah, but he does not give rise to dark-skinned Africans. The other two sons of Ham, Cush and Put, father the African nations of the Bible. Cush and Put, however, were notably NOT cursed. In the words of Felder, "Into the seventeenth century the idea persisted that the blackness of Africans was due to a curse, and that idea reinforced and sanctioned the enslavement of blacks" (Felder 1991:132).

My mother, her mother, whole generations of Black Catholics were told that their blackness was a curse. Like Butler, we were forced to wonder whether we really are as good as Whites. How long, after all, was the curse supposed to last? Perhaps by now the curse has worn off. Maybe today, so many generations after the flood, we might be almost as good as Whites. And our tradition of accepting whatever our priests and nuns told us unquestioningly kept us from looking for ourselves. If we had just opened the Bible and thought about it, we might have been spared years of heartache.

A while ago I was teaching a class on the history of oppression. I asked my all-white class what they knew about the curse of Ham. No one in the room had heard of it. At first I was surprised. Slowly, however, it dawned on me that they had no reason to know it. In all their years, no one had ever told them that they'd been cursed by God for something over which they have no control. What a luxury to grow up that way.

* * *

How often have the letters of Paul been used to keep Blacks AND women from participating fully in society? As recently as last Sunday we endured those dreaded words, "Wives, be obedient to your husbands." After Mass, I mentioned jokingly that there must have been a typo, 'wives' and 'husbands' got switched somehow. One of the men overheard me – one who's respected by the parishioners as being educated and informed on spiritual matters – and commented, "Here we go again, re-writing scripture!" Ironic, considering the source of those particular passages.

There is doubt, it turns out, about the authorship of the household codes, or *Haustafeln*, of the Pauline epistles. Paul himself probably never wrote the 'obedience' codes. According to Clarice Martin (1991), the *Haustafeln* were introduced into the epistles after Paul's death to curb the zeal of the early Christian converts. The enthusiasm of women and slaves disrupted quiet, efficient Greco-Roman households and threatened the patriarchal status quo, so much so that, rather than welcoming Christian missionaries, communities began trying to drive them away. The *Haustafeln*, written after 70 CE, were meant to help restore order and reinforce patriarchal control. They were designed to reassure communities that Christianity was not a threat to the government.

The bottom line is this – the 'obedience' segments of Paul's epistles were probably not written by Paul at all. "[T]he *Haustafeln* and the letters in which they are found are not Pauline, but deutero-Pauline. The question of whether the *Haustafeln* are Pauline is, of course, linked to the question of the authenticity of Colossians, Ephesians, and 1 Peter. I would argue that Colossians and Ephesians are deutero-Pauline, that is, written by circles of Paul's students on the model of the Pauline letter" (Martin 1991:207).

All those centuries of biblical justification for the institution of slavery were based on false premises. No curse of Ham, and no message from Paul. They all became part of a racist political ideology designed to ensure White superiority over Blacks, and male superiority over women.

Racism. It's not simply politically incorrect. It's more than just a bad habit. Racism unlocks the door to a multitude of other sins. When we view our neighbors through the lens of racism, we deny them their humanity. Racism warps every other aspect of life too. It promotes the false belief that we are better than other human beings, closer to God, more deserving of rewards, that salvation is easier for us. The opposite, however, is really true. When we allow ourselves to fall prey to racist notions, we grow farther from God. We step farther away from the path of justice. We ourselves have become less human. We don't become better, we become worse than the ones we oppress. That's one reason why racism is such a terrible sin.

The National Conference of Catholic Bishops has this to say about it: "Racism is not merely one sin among many; it is a radical evil that divides the human family"(NCCB 1979:10). Bryan Massingale points out that racism is more than simply the personal attitudes and behaviors of one individual toward another. It also encompasses covert acts of institutionalized racism embedded in society, including structures that enhance the success of majority groups while restricting that of minorities. So racism can be unconscious, unintentional, woven into the very fabric of society, including marginalization and exclusion of oppressed groups of people (Massingale 1998:156-157).

Sin is more than just an individual action. Participating in racist structures or policies is also sinful. The Whites who fled the cities during the 1960s and 1970s to avoid having Black neighbors, therefore, were committing a sin. The real estate agent who shows a Black family only the homes in mixed or Black neighborhoods is also sinning, as is the banker who arranges for a Black person's loan to have a higher interest rate than a White person with the same credit rating.

James Cone pushes the envelope even farther. It is not enough to recognize that racism occurs and to avoid it on an individual level. To be truly Christian, one must join the ranks of the oppressed and fight side-by-side against oppression (Cone 1997:135).

Racism has so warped our minds that one can hardly talk about it in a college classroom without the students becoming defensive, divisive, and argumentative. Every year it's the same story. Whenever I bring up the topic in an all White or nearly all White classroom, my students first attempt to deny that racism exists at all. Many of them have Black friends or Black neighbors. Some consider themselves minorities since they attended schools in which Whites were outnumbered by Blacks and Hispanics. Then, they try to find examples of what they call 'reverse racism' – Black people taking advantage of affirmative action policies, or White people who didn't get into a selective college because someone Black 'who didn't meet the admission criteria' took away their spots. Before you know it, the students are arguing over the existence of racism rather than examining the data critically.

Just last week, one of my students – in a homogeneous classroom of 25 White freshmen – tried to convince the rest of the class that most of the first-year seats in college admissions this year were taken up by minority students. I asked him to glance around the room – how can he look at his classmates and still believe what he was saying? Yet still he persisted in the argument. He'd read it in a newspaper article.

Cyprian Davis discusses his experiences with racism while teaching in the seminary: "Liberal seminary or conservative, all male or mixed, politically correct or fundamentalist, a classroom of White students in this country can rarely treat race and related issues with equanimity or objectivity. History should provide the perfect background for controversial topics, for distance lends enchantment and age adds a patina that softens the harshness and relieves the glare. [. . .] Unless we wish upon future priests a frontal lobotomy that will take away anxiety and remove all tensions, we must allow them to face the specters and the shades of the past. We can exorcise the demons only when we call their names" (Davis 1997:51).

CONCLUSION

"Most Black Catholics would also agree that [many people] fail to understand the deep commitment in faith that has made Black Catholics remain rooted in the Catholic Church" (Davis 1998:282).

* * *

Faith. There are more than two and a half million Black Catholics in America. Black Catholics, despite the racism of various priests, despite institutionalized racism, despite the lack of Black role models, are among the most devoted. When I left the Church in 1985, I thought the Church was made up of the Father Bills, Father Graysons, and Mrs. Elrods. The sisters who saved us in 1968 were long gone. But truly good Catholics are still out there, and they are probably in the majority. My time at St. Sebastian's has proven that.

Racism is one problem among many in the Church. What about pedophilia? An appalling, horrifying statement of priests' objectification of the most innocent and helpless victims. In a way, though, the pedophilia problem is very much like the problem of racism. In both cases, there is careless disregard of those most vulnerable. And in both cases, it isn't the priests who are most to blame. It's the bishops who, in full knowledge of their priests' offenses, turned their backs on the people. That's why my sister decided to leave the Church. The tenuous hold it may have had on her prior to publication of the pedophilia scandal is broken for all time, and she's decided not to raise her children as Catholics largely because of it. She's not the only one.

But for every pedophile, there are one hundred caring priests who may be saving lives. For every racist, there may be another hundred priests struggling to see past the veil of oppression. For every Father George, there's a Father Richard somewhere. For every Father Grayson, there's a Sol. For every Mrs. Elrod, there's a nun out there saving children, or a Martha devoted to helping the children of her parish find a healthy place for themselves and answers to their questions about faith.

My mother may not have harmed us in 1967, but without the sisters she may have attracted the attention of some DCF caseworker who would have taken us away from her. We could have ended up in foster care, separated from one another. We wouldn't have had access to an education in a Catholic school, we wouldn't have had a chance to earn scholarships for college. As it is, all five of us finished college, and most of us went on to earn advanced degrees. With all its faults, we owe much of our success to the Church that kept providing us with opportunities to find funding and support of some sort.

The Church still does more good than harm. The Catholic colleges and seminaries are making room for the teachings of Copeland, Phelps, Davis, Conwill, Massingale, Cone, Hayes, Felder, Martin, and a host of other scholars whose research elucidates the experiences of Blacks in the

Church and the sin of racism and sexism. It's a slow process – it seems glacial at times – but we're moving in the right direction. And the oppressors of the world are becoming fewer and losing their audiences. They're still out there, confusing people and causing trouble. They're a disturbing element of the Church. Their ideas may never die out completely. But as long as we have the Copelands, Sols, Davis's, and Sister Mary Pauls, we have hope. We have a great deal to be happy about.

What about my mother Beatrice? The damage done to her self-image in the name of Catholicism has seemed unforgivable to me at times. The Church wasn't the only party responsible, but, since she gave her trust to it, it may be the guiltiest. But the Church also gave her a lifeline. She was devastated by my father's abandonment. My grandmother worried that she might take her own life. She was even more worried that she'd take us with her. And it was the Church that gave her the strength to go on. Her faith may have been the only thing that saved her – and us.

Today, more than forty years after my parents separated, my mother lives alone. She struggles with agoraphobia as well as schizophrenia, and discourages visits from us although she insists on regular phone calls. The only thing she has to live for is prayer, and she prays several rosaries every day. A priest visits her once a month to give her Holy Communion. The only television program she watches is weekly Mass on Sunday mornings. Without the Church, she would have nothing.

I may still leave the Church. The Father Georges of the world are sometimes too tiresome to bear. And when I see the effect of his behavior on John and his family, on the entire parish, I get angry. When I think about the young boys who were abused by the very people they may have trusted the most, I become furious. But I can't expect the Church to be perfect. Julia was right. *WE* are the solution to the problems of the Church. If I decide to go, it'll be a leave-taking from St. Sebastian's. I don't think I could ever walk completely away from the Church that made me what I am.

In the words of Bryan Massingale (1997:95): "[I] hope that the American Catholic Moral community not only can be, but will be, enriched by the insights of its fellow believers and citizens of African descent, so that one day it will be true that the African American experience and U.S. Catholic moral theology are 'strangers and aliens no longer.'"

WORK CITED

Agence France Presse (2004). 'Vatican Drops Objections to
    Altar Girls and Happier Masses'. International News,
    April 23, p. A2.

Beecher, P.A. (translated by M.E. Smith) 2006. 'Homily.'
    *The Catholic Encyclopedia Volume VII, The Online
    Edition.* Retrieved August 27, 2006.
    <http://www.newadvent.org/>

Bureau of Justice Statistics (2006). 'Prison Statistics'. U.S.
    Department of Justice. Retrieved September 17, 2006.
    <http://www.ojp.usdoj.gov/bjs/prisons.htm>

Butler, Octavia E. (2005). 'Positive Obsession.' Pp. 123-136
    in *Bloodchild and Other Stories*, by Octavia Butler. New
    York: Seven Stories Press.

Catechism of the Catholic Church (2006), paragraph 1304.
    Retrieved September 5, 2006.
    <http://www.vatican.va/archive/catechism/p2s2c1a2.
    htm.>

Cone, James (1997). *God of the Oppressed*, revised edition.
    New York: Orbis Books.

Conwill, Giles (1998). 'Black Catechesis.' Pp. 199-231 in
    *Taking Down Our Harps. Black Catholics in the United
    States,* edited by Diana L. Hayes and Cyprian Davis,
    O.S.B. New York: Orbis Books.

Copeland, M. Shawn (1998). 'Method in Emerging Black
    Catholic Theology.' Pp. 120-144 in *Taking Down Our
    Harps. Black Catholics in the United States,* edited by
    Diana L. Hayes and Cyprian Davis, O.S.B. New York:
    Orbis Books.

Daifallah, Adam (2003). 'Bush: Michigan's Affirmative Action
    Policy Unfair.' *The New York Sun*, January 16, A1.

Davis, Cyprian, O.S.B., D.Hist.Sc. (1997). 'Reclaiming the Spirit: On Teaching Church History: 'Why Can't They Be More Like Us?" Pp. 43-53 in *Black and Catholic: The Challenge and Gift of Black Folk* edited by Jamie Phelps, O.P. Wisconsin: Marquette University Press.

Davis, Cyprian , O.S.B., D.Hist.Sc. (1998). 'Speaking the Truth.' Pp. 281-285 in *Taking Down Our Harps. Black Catholics in the United States,* edited by Diana L. Hayes and Cyprian Davis, O.S.B. New York: Orbis Books.

Driscoll, John T. (2006). 'Miracle.' *The Catholic Encyclopedia, Volume X, The Online Edition.* Retrieved August 27, 2006.<http://www.newadvent.org/cathen/10338a.htm>

Felder, Cain Hope. (1991). 'Race, Racism, and the Biblical Narratives.' Pp. 127-145 in *Stony the Road We Trod. African American Biblical Interpretation,* edited by Cain Hope Felder. Minnesota: Fortress Press.

Hayes, Diana (1998). 'And When We Speak: To be Black, Catholic, and Womanist.' Pp. 102-119 in *Taking Down Our Harps. Black Catholics in the United States,* edited by Diana L. Hayes and Cyprian Davis, O.S.B. New York: Orbis Books.

Hilgers, Joseph (translated by Michael C. Tinkler) 2006. 'Index of Prohibited Books.' *The Catholic Encyclopedia Volume VII, The Online Edition.* Retrieved August 27, 2006. <http://www.newadvent.org/>.

Louis, E. (2002). 'Mr. Lott and the Party of Ideas.' *The New York Sun.* December 10, Editorial and Opinion, p. 6.

Martin, Clarice (1991). 'The *Haustafeln* (Household Codes) in African American Biblical Interpretation: 'Free Slaves' and 'Subordinate Women''. Pp. 206-231 in *Stony the Road We Trod: African American Biblical Interpretation,* edited by Cain Hope Felder. Minnesota: Fortress Press.

Massingale, Bryan S.T.D. (1997). 'The African American Experience and U.S. Roman Catholic Ethics. Strangers and Aliens No Longer?' Pp. 79-101 in *Black and Catholic: The Challenge and Gift of Black,* edited by Jamie T. Phelps, O.P. Wisconsin: Marquette University Press.

Massingale, Bryan S.T.D. (1998). 'The Case for Catholic Support. Catholic Social Ethics and Environmental Justice.' Pp. 147-162 in *Taking Down Our Harps. Black Catholics in the United States,* edited by Diana L. Hayes and Cyprian Davis, O.S.B. New York: Orbis Books.

McGreevy, John T. (1996). Parish Boundaries. The Catholic Encounter with Race in the Twentieth Century Urban North. Chicago: University of Chicago Press.

National Conference of Catholic Bishops (1979). 'Brothers and Sisters to Us.' Washington, D.C.

Newshog (2006). "Catholic Issues 'Fatwa' for Dan Brown's Head. May 24, 2006. Retrieved August 10, 2006. <http://cernigsnewshog.blogspot.com/2006/05/catholic-issues-fatwa-for-dan-browns.html>

O'Malley, Vincent J. C.M. (2001). *Saints of Africa.* Indiana: Our Sunday Visitor Publishing Division.

Phelps, Jamie T., O.P. (1997). 'African American Catholic Struggles, Contributions, Gifts.' Pp. 17-42 in *Black and Catholic: The Challenge and Gift of Black Folk,* edited by Jamie T. Phelps, O.P. Wisconsin: Marquette University Press.

Phelps, Jamie T., O.P. (1998). 'Inculturating Jesus: A Search for Dynamic Images for the Mission of the Church among African Americans.' Pp. 68-101 in *Taking Down Our Harps. Black Catholics in the United States,* edited by Diana L. Hayes and Cyprian Davis, O.S.B. New York: Orbis Books.

Raboteau, Albert (1974, 2004). Slave Religion: The 'Invisible Institution' in the Antebellum South. Updated Edition. Oxford: Oxford University Press.

Raspberry, William (2005). 'Lynching Apologies a Good Start' *The Times Union*, June 20, A47.

Shannon, David T. (1991). 'An Ante-bellum Sermon: A Resource for an African American Hermeneutic.' Pp. 98-123 in *Stony the Road We Trod: African American Biblical Interpretation*, edited by Cain Hope Felder. Minnesota: Fortress Press.

Snowden, Frank (1991). *Before Color Prejudice. The Ancient View of Blacks*. Cambridge: Harvard University Press.

Tardy, Jo Anne (2006). A Light Will Rise in the Darkness. Illinois: Acta Publications.

Trower, Cathy and Richard Chait (2002). 'Faculty Diversity. Too Little for Too Long'. *Harvard Magazine*. Retrieved August 27, 2006. <http://www.harvardmagazine.com/on-line/030218.html>.

U.S. Census Bureau (2006). Retrieved 12 September 2006. <http://www.census.gov>

Women Priests (2006). "The Case for Ordaining Women in The Catholic Church." Retrieved 27 August 2006. <http://www.womenpriests.org/pdebate.asp>

Word, Ron (2006). '3 Convicted in Xbox Video Game Slayings'. *Yahoo News*. Retrieved July 31, 2006. <http://news.yahoo.com/s/ap/20060725/ap_on_re_us/video_game_slayings>.

Gift Aid item

20 **10058737** 4749

Why I Left the Church
Why I Came Back, and
Why I Just Might Leave Again
by Jean K. Douglas

The 1960s, 70s, and 80s were turbulent decades for the Catholic Church as it struggled to navigate the waters of racial injustice and the woman's movement. Many studies document those troubled times from the outsider's perspective, but almost none feature that of the insider. Douglas provides her readers with a new lens through which to view parochial teachings on race relations, integration, and gender roles. Her touching account of the ways priests, nuns, and her mother influenced her formative years reveals for the first time the conflicts faced by a Black girl trying to come to terms with her faith.

"*. . . engaging and elegant in its style.*"
Dr. Cecilia Moore
Department of History
University of Dayton

'*With just the right balance of affection and anger, Douglas poignantly shows the paradox of a Church that both blesses and curses: healing with the love of Christ on the one hand, and wounding with the evil of racism on the other. In our increasingly global world, her message is timely and urgent. This book brought me to tears with its beauty and pathos. The Church better hope she doesn't leave again. It needs her.*"

Dr. Susan Peppers-Bates
Department of Philosophy, Women and Gender Studies Program
Stetson University

Ⓡ **Oxfam**
£1•99

Winner of the 2006
Royal Palm Literary Award

U.S. $17.99/Canada $21.99
ISBN-13: 978-0-9789635-0-7
ISBN-10: 0-9789635-0-4

5 1 7 9 9

Fortuity Press
www.fortuitypress.com

9 780978 963507